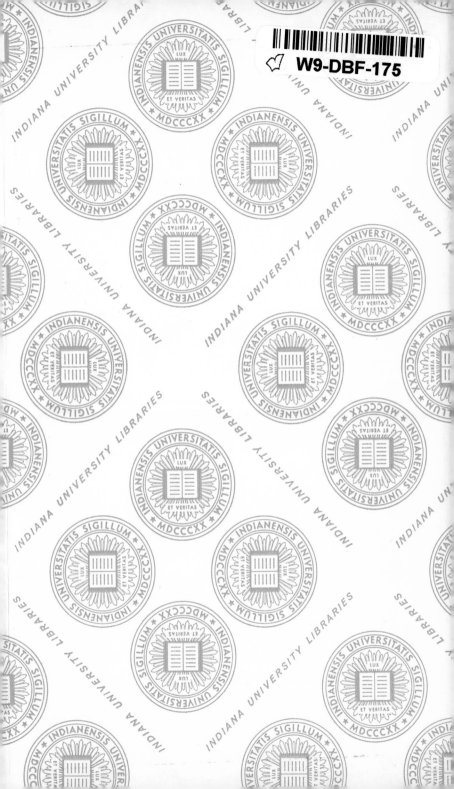

ADJUSTMENT PSYCHOLOGY

A HUMAN VALUE
APPROACH

ADJUSTMENT PSYCHOLOGY

A HUMAN VALUE APPROACH

RONAL G. POLAND, Ph.D.

Psychologist in private practice, Denver, Colorado;
formerly Lecturer and Consultant,
Division of Continuing Education,
University of Colorado, Boulder

NANCY D. SANFORD, R.N., M.S.

Instructor of Psychiatric Nursing, St. Luke's Hospital
School of Nursing, Denver, Colorado; Consultant in Psychiatric
Nursing, Group Dynamics, and Communication

THE C. V. MOSBY COMPANY

Saint Louis   1971

Copyright © 1971 by The C. V. Mosby Company

Printed in the United States of America

Standard Book Number 8016-3954-9

Library of Congress Catalog Card Number 70-138864

Distributed in Great Britain by Henry Kimpton, London

PREFACE

This book is designed for the undergraduate who may or may not have had an introductory course in psychology. It presents a variety of material about human behavior. Some readers will not agree with everything that has been written here. It is not a book filled with material to which readers must agree; it is designed to provoke discussion. It is made up of some material that is reasonably well supported by research findings in the behaviorial sciences and some material of a more speculative nature.

On the more speculative side, emphasis has been placed on the need for individuals to develop what has been called a sense of personal identity. To "know thyself" appears to be an increasingly useful admonition because of great and rapid changes taking place in the social and cultural environment in which we all live.

Because our environment moves in the direction of greater complexity, it becomes more difficult to comprehend. It offers few substantial anchors for the individual. What anchors there are may shift from time to time and many relationships and ties can be viewed as transitory, ephemeral, and fragile. Conceivably, it may be that the only permanent relationship one has is the relationship with oneself. Yet, there remains the prospect of each person's having a few reasonably durable and intimate relationships with a limited number of other people. The quality of the interaction one has with another, however, may be based upon the quality and depth of one's relationship with himself. Perhaps this book will be useful in that respect. Perhaps this book can assist the individual in his attempts to know about himself and to know some of the components of workable and satisfying relationships with a few other people.

Readers of this book will find a number of pages that call for written responses. It is not an absolute requirement that they write out what is asked of them, but the writing is keyed to the material in the book and should help in understanding that material. It may be that some instructors will want to use the written material in research projects. At the beginning of each chapter are brief pieces of fiction that relate to the content of the chapter. Sometimes the connection between the fiction and the content is obvious and direct. Sometimes the connection is ambiguous, and the ambiguity may facilitate or provoke discussion.

We wish to thank the following individuals for their help in the development and writing of this book: Lillian DeYoung, Jane Helmer, Ultima Wells, Robert F. Mager, Fred McKinney, Larry Currier, George Hartlaub, Richard B. Cattell, and Henry V. Z. Cobb.

Ronal G. Poland
Nancy D. Sanford

CONTENTS

ADJUSTMENT PSYCHOLOGY

A HUMAN VALUE
APPROACH

1

INFANCY

She was pregnant. She didn't want to be but she was. She had been pregnant for a month and nothing showed; but at night she had dreams of being large and awkward, cow-like, grotesque. She hated the dreams. Inside her, the month-old embryo was alive in the darkness, less than an inch long, with one head and one torso and two pairs of limbs that could be legs and arms or fins. Its unfinished heart was beating.

The baby was born on a Monday morning; and when the father heard it was a girl, he didn't know, for several seconds, whether to be happy or angry or relieved. He decided to be happy. He smiled when the nurse held up his first born for him to see.

The infant was ten minutes old; but inside her tiny ovaries, there were half a million cells resting in place, each a potential female egg. Thirteen years after this girl's birth, one of those half million cells would leave one of the two ovaries to travel through a fallopian tube to the uterus. For a forty-eight hour period every month that thirteen-year-old would be capable of becoming a mother herself.

She didn't become a mother until she was twenty-three. For ten years her body had formed one egg a month. Each egg had deteriorated and had been washed away by the process of menstruation. The one hundred twentieth egg was fertilized, and nine months later she gave birth to a boy. Now the boy was fifteen days old and hungry. She prepared herself for nursing him. She unbuttoned her blouse, exposed her breast, and lifted the infant out of his crib. When she picked him up, he automatically moved his head toward her breast and his lips smacked open and shut until they touched the enlarged nipple. As he suckled, he looked up into his mother's face. She looked down at him and smiled.

She loved him. She loved to touch his small face with her fingertips. With a smile, she hold his hand and counted the fingers and marveled at the small and beautifully formed fingernails. When she bathed him, she laughed softly, sometimes with an almost sensual delight.

When he was three weeks old, she took him with her when she went to the market to get him more food. At the store, she saw people she didn't know. She wanted to run up to them and hold her baby out for them to see. She wanted to shout, "Look!! Look at my baby!" but she never did.

At night, when she was alone with her thoughts in the darkness, she wondered about him and about herself. "He cannot live without me," she said to the darkness.

He was a month old when she took him to the clinic. She undressed him for the doctor. Stepping back, she watched the physician lean over her son who lay on his back on the examination table. As the doctor tapped and probed and listened and watched, she felt uncomfortable, vaguely disturbed. "He's got to be all right," she said to herself. "I cannot live without him."

When the doctor was finished, he straightened up and looked at the mother. He smiled and said, "Well, your baby looks fine. I guess he's inherited the good things." The mother relaxed.

She took him to the clinic again when he was six months old. He sat up on the examining table this time and watched the doctor closely. After the examination, his mother dressed him, and he made soft sounds as he put his fingers in his mouth.

When he was a year old, he tried to eat the single candle on his birthday cake. His mother took the candle away. He looked at her for a moment, and then he reached his hand out and pushed his fingers down through the cake frosting. Lifting his hand out of the frosting, he stuck his fingers into his mouth and gurgled.

He could walk strongly now, going up and down stairs, and talking when he didn't have something in his mouth. The cat stayed away from him because he'd bitten her tail three times. His father, chewing on a yellow pencil, watched the infant boy and laughed. The boy looked at his father and laughed back.

Hereditary factors begin with germ cells. Germ cells are called that not because they carry sickness but because they carry life. The male germ cell (a sperm cell) penetrates and unites with a female germ cell (an egg cell). This is the moment of conception; the time when life begins for a new individual. The sperm and the egg merge to form a single cell called a zygote.

The sperm and the egg both contain chromosomes. As with shoes and gloves, chromosomes come in pairs. In each egg and each sperm there are twenty-three pairs of chromosomes or forty-six in all.

Chromosomes carry many thousands of genes. Each gene is responsible for a particular physical trait or characteristic. Several genes may combine to produce one trait.

Genes work in pairs too, although not in some equal way. In a pair of genes, one comes from the father and one comes from the mother.

Each gene is a molecule composed mostly of deoxyribonucleic acid or DNA. These DNA molecules produce enzymes, which control the formation of proteins within a cell. By this control, genes are able to determine the kinds of tissues formed to make the body.

Centuries ago, and even in recent times, there were kings, shahs, and emperors who banished one wife and married another because the first wife produced only female children. Even now, there are men (not usually kings, though) who change wives in order to have a male heir. You may know some father who feels dissatisfied with his wife because she has not given him a boy child.

It does not make much sense to change wives or be dissatisfied because she has not brought forth a male child. It is the father, by way of his own genes, who decides the sex of the children.

The sex of an individual is determined by genes. The sex-determining chromosomes of the mother are all the same kind of chromosomes, whereas the sex determining chromosomes of the father are both X and Y chromosomes. Thus, if a sperm cell carrying an X chromosome unites with the egg cell, the child will be a girl; if the sperm cell carries a Y chromosome, the child will be a boy. So, it is the male who determines the sex of the child and not the female.

■ The child will tend to inherit characteristics of the parent of the same sex.

TRUE   (TURN TO PAGE 9.)

FALSE   (TURN TO PAGE 12.)

3

Genes work in pairs, although not always in equal ways. If a woman whose ancestors came from Norway marries a man whose forefathers came from Africa, the children will probably be more Afro-American than Norwegian-American in appearance. If a Japanese-American marries an English-American, the offspring will probably look slightly more Oriental than Caucasian.

Geneticists maintain that when (not if) all the races of the world intermix all human beings will be light brown with dark hair and dark eyes. It is relatively easy to predict how people will look then, because genes work in ways that are predictable.

Genes and chromosomes determine how a person looks. Genes and chromosomes also determine, to some degree, how a person behaves. The study of the relationship between genetics and behavior was once called psychogenetics, but now the term *behavioral genetics* has become more widely used.

Behavioral geneticists focus their main attention on the sorts of behavior that may be inherited. They must also take into account and know about behavior that results from experiences with the environment in which the individual lives. According to the present state of scientific development, it is difficult for behavioral geneticists (and anyone else, for that matter) to clearly distinguish between many behaviors that are *acquired* or learned and behaviors that are *innate* or inherited. Some behavioral patterns are combinations of the two.

When a baby is 7 or 8 days old, he begins to show an important response, the *rooting* response. This was identified by Dr. Rene Spitz, a man who spent a lifetime specializing in studies of early infancy. Changing a baby's body position causes the inner ear balance mechanism to be tipped in a new direction. The slight and temporary disturbance of the inner ear is one of the factors that bring this complex rooting response. Rooting takes place when the infant, searching for nourishment, turns his head to one side and snaps his lips open and shut.

When the infant finds the nipple and begins to suck, he can feel the breast against his face. He experiences the sensation of contact.

It is a physical response, a complex and reflexive behavior that can be seen in every human infant. Not only is rooting physical, but it has great psychological importance.

The rooting response sets in motion a two-way contact. The infant has a relationship with his mother and the mother has a relationship with her infant. Spitz calls this reciprocal contact *the primal dialogue*. The dialogue becomes as necessary to the life of the infant as food.

Part of the primal dialogue involves the baby's sight. As the infant's vision improves and he looks up into his mother's face, there is also a sensation of contact but of a different kind. The infant, in time, learns the difference. The child can be removed from the breast, thus breaking one form of contact; but while his mother's face is still in full view, another sort of contact remains.

The infant must have food or he will starve to death. The infant must also experience the primal dialogue or else he may die.

When a baby is born, the only finished part of that new being is the hereditary portion. All the genes and chromosomes, all the spiraled molecules of DNA, are there, but the baby is incomplete. The newborn child is unfinished physically. For instance, after birth, the bones of the skull and the teeth continue to grow and develop.

After birth, the baby must live for months before the realization comes that he is an individual. The newborn child has no experience in sensing the separateness that exists between himself and all other people and things in his environment. The blanket he holds is as much a part of him as his hand. Mother is not another person but is a part of him, and he is a part of her for almost a year. He may not sense much about his own physical uniqueness or develop much awareness of his own body until almost two years have passed. By then he will be aware of much more than simple feelings of comfort or discomfort.

As the child learns to talk, the self-awareness becomes more apparent. Self-awareness develops as he learns the meaning of his name and the names of others; he learns to distinguish between what is his and what is not his.

Gradually he recognizes differences between himself and others. He uses such words as "I," "me," "mine" to differentiate himself from others.

The self eventually comes to be a combination of the person's thoughts and feelings, his view of what he is, what he has been, and what he hopes to become. This self represents the person's awareness of his own personality.

■ The development of the self is greatly influenced by other people.

TRUE   (TURN TO PAGE 11.)

FALSE   (TURN TO PAGE 15.)

Infancy is the first of eight stages of development, and it covers the time from birth to about 2 years of age. The stage of infancy is sometimes called the oral stage because the infant's mouth is the instrument of survival and the tool for achieving pleasure.

From the moment of birth, the infant's needs are primarily biological. The infant needs food and water, oxygen and warmth. If these needs are met, he will be comfortable and happy; if not, he will be anxious, frustrated, and then angry. Because the infant's first feelings of comfort are obtained through feeding and sucking, food becomes associated with love. The child receives as much love from bottle feeding as from breast feeding only as long as he is held while taking the bottle feeding.

Because the mother usually feeds the child, he begins to associate mother with the relief of his needs. If his needs are met consistently, he learns to trust that he will be cared for when necessary.

The development of trust is a critical achievement during infancy.

Trust is a feeling that the world is a dependable and nice place and that the people in it are usually warm and friendly.

If the needs of the infant are not met and his distress signals are ignored, he will have a feeling that the world is an unpleasant place, that the people in it are unloving.

Mother provides his first social contact with another person. He begins to trust mother, who becomes the object of his feelings of affection. The capacity to feel affection develops out of the positive effects of this first relationship. If the infant does not receive a positive mothering experience, he will find it difficult to have or show loving feelings to other people. If his experiences are mostly positive, he will come to trust people and consider them well intentioned.

■ In later adult life the child who accomplishes the task of developing a sense of trust will continue to receive pleasure from oral activities.

TRUE   (TURN TO PAGE 10.)

FALSE   (TURN TO PAGE 13.)

During the first few years of life, the child eagerly puts things into his mouth and into his stomach. Sometimes infants with upset stomachs are x-rayed, and physicians can see pins, bolts, pieces of toys, and bits of wood in the stomach.

During the first years of life, the child introjects words and actions, ideas and concepts; but unlike food and debris, these never show up on x-ray film.

The child will *introject* all kinds of attitudes and ideas from his parents. He will cooperatively go along with them for several years. But then cooperation is interrupted at about age 3. At that time the child becomes resistant. This resistance to the ideas and rules that the parents have is sometimes called *negativism*.

Not only is negativism normal, but it seems necessary at this age.

By being temporarily resistant to his parents' ideas of how life ought to be lived, the infant is establishing himself as a real person rather than as merely an extension of his parents or a thing they happen to own.

If the negativism of early years becomes fixed in the behavior of the person, if it becomes a generalized sort of response to parents, the child may be working at being unlike the parents. The process can sometimes be an interesting one. If, for instance, the father is a careless, over-the-limit speeder, a poor driver, the son, negativistically, may evolve into a careful, law-abiding driver. If the mother is a real shrew, her daughter may act like an angel. If, however, the parent is studious and generally logical, the child may, in being negativistic, develop an antipathy toward schools and thrive on being illogical.

If the negativism of early years becomes fixed in behavior, the child loses as much independence and self-direction in his life as if he were a carbon copy of his parents. If the child strives to be unlike his parents, he loses freedom just as much as he would if he chose to imitate those parents as closely as possible.

How can this affect you? Think carefully about the way in which you live. Then, on a blank page, write down two characteristics of your living pattern. After giving the matter some thought, explain how these characteristics came to be yours. Did you get them by way of introjection or negativism?

What you have been reading for the last several pages is overly simplified. People are more than a collection of introjections and negativisms. Yet, what we introject and what we become negativistic about have a profound influence on our lives.

From the moment of conception and on through childhood and adulthood, each of us is faced with the problem of being someone.

This is not the same as being something. To be something is to be a lawyer, a mother, a pilot, an artist, or a teacher. To be someone is to be a person; and we are all confronted, much of the time, with the problem of deciding what sort of person to be.

There are, basically, three ways of being someone, three paths to choose from:

1. To be like one's parents (introjection)
2. To be unlike one's parents (negativism)
3. To be one's own self

We can and do choose to be the way we are. How and why we choose are complicated by matters that involve motivations, certain rewards for our behavior, and the way in which we handle ourselves when we interact with other people.

Turn to Chapter 2, page 16.

Well, in a way you are correct. The child will inherit certain body structures and functions appropriate to his sex.

However, each individual receives a unique combination of chromosomes and genes from each parent. Usually a child receives about equal numbers of chromosomes from all four grandparents. Consequently, the child will inherit some (but by *no* means the majority) of the characteristics of the parent of the same sex.

Return to page 3 and select another answer.

Correct. Even the most mature adult generally receives a great deal of pleasure from using the mouth for eating, drinking, smoking, and love making.

If the infant was fed regularly and with warmth and affection, he learns to tolerate stress without excessive frustration. He also learns to enjoy pleasure of the mouth without going to excessives of eating and drinking.

Persons who successfully achieve a sense of trust will usually be optimistic and loving adults.

GO ON TO PAGE 7.

Yes. The kinds of experiences the child has with other people will definitely affect his perception of self. From other people the child forms a picture of what he is, what he has been like in the past, and how he will be in future. No one experience will determine self-awareness; each experience gains meaning and impact from all those that preceded it.

If the child receives praise, love, and attention from his parents most of the time, he will see himself as a desirable, loving, and lovable person.

The child who has many experiences of rejection, deprivation, and criticism will see himself as undesirable, unworthy, and unlovable.

If others respect his physical and mental abilities, the child will feel capable. If the child is told he is not capable, he will tend to perceive himself that way even if, in fact, he has average abilities. If the child inherits physical characteristics that are rewarded by this society, such as being tall, slim, and coordinated, he will probably be considered capable and thus feel capable. Mental abilities are rewarded most if the person also has physical and social skills.

The ability to respect self is dependent on how we feel we are rated by others, especially people who we believe are important. In childhood this seems to be the case. In adulthood, we strive for independence from the evaluations of other people.

CONTINUE TO PAGE 6.

You are right, the statement is false. The combination of genes and chromosomes a person receives is quite variable. Each mother and father have more than 8 million different possible combinations of traits to pass on to their children.

Although a person receives chromosomes and genes from his parents, the various combinations from a pool of billions of possibilities cause individuals to be both like and unlike other members of their family.

NOTE: At least two great benefits come to all of us because we know that there are such things as hereditary factors.

One of these is the field of genetics. The scientific study of heredity has led to better and more plentiful food for mankind. It has helped in the understanding of the 500 diseases transmitted by hereditary means. Genetics has, within recent years, given us a deeper understanding of the force we call life.

In addition, the mere existence of genetics has provided nearly everyone (except geneticists) with an easy and general answer to the understanding of all kinds of behavior. It does not seem to matter that the easy answers can often be wrong. Many people observe and study their own behavior or the behavior of others and attribute the behavior to heredity. Often someone will say, "Well, it's in the blood," or, "I was born that way," or "He inherited that from his father." A person can be a "born leader" or a "born loser," and there are supposed to be such things as the "instinct of mother love" and so on. Such comments refer to behavior or existence that is not inherited.

Write down, on a blank page, some of your inherited characteristics. On another page, write down some characteristics that you have but did not inherit from your parents.

THEN, TURN TO PAGE 14.

Wrong. Don't you enjoy using your mouth for kissing? If you do not enjoy that, perhaps you like good food.

The mature adult continues to derive pleasure from using the mouth for eating, drinking, love making. However, if the adult did not develop a sense of trust, he may use oral gratifications to excess, such as overeating (and becoming obese) or drinking too much (and becoming an alcoholic). In such cases, the person is said to be fixated at the oral stage, or unable to progress to more mature levels of behavior.

Persons who do not achieve a sense of trust tend to be pessimistic as adults. Because of poor relationships leading to a poor sense of trust, these people may expect and demand love, attention, and dependency as adults.

START AGAIN ON PAGE 6.

In listing some of your inherited characteristics you might have put down your eye color, your blood type, and your level of intelligence. You would have been correct on the first two and partly wrong on the last one.

In listing some characteristics you did not inherit, you might have put down the color of your shoes, the language you speak, and your level of intelligence. You would, again, be correct on the first two and partly wrong on the last one.

Some of the characteristics you have are clearly the result of genetic transmission. There are characteristics that have been transmitted by the genes you received from your parents. Other characteristics you have are obviously not inherited. Still others are a mixture of the two. For instance, your level of intelligence is based on what you have inherited *and* on what you have experienced in your life. You are made up of a package of hereditary factors combined with environmental experiences.

NOW TURN TO PAGE 4.

Think it over. Do you perceive yourself according to how others react to you and how you think they feel about you?

A term for this reaction is reflected appraisal. The appraisal of others is reflected onto the self.

Most children receive contradictory appraisals of self. However, the child of age 2 or 3 will probably consider himself "good me" or "bad me" according to the reflected appraisal of significant people (parents in particular) in his life.

Select the other answer on page 5.

2

CHILDHOOD
AND
ADOLESCENCE

When the child was old enough, his mother began to teach him to go to the bathroom. He didn't care much for the new rules, until he saw his father urinate. After that, he rapidly developed good control of his excretory functions; but, sometimes, he relieved himself in ways and places that seemed designed to embarrass his mother. Once, standing in the sunlight and smiling at the mail man, who laughed out loud, he urinated on the front steps.

He was playing outside one day in late autumn when the first snow of the season began to fall. Not knowing what it was, he started to go indoors to tell his mother about the soft white stuff. He changed his mind and ran to tell the boy down the block. When he got there, he found that no one was home, so he walked around in the falling snow, felt it on his face and grabbed at flakes as they fell past him. Soon, the ground was covered with a thin layer of snow and he saw that he made tracks wherever he walked. He walked and ran and walked some more. He looked behind himself from time to time to see the long, wavering trail of footprints he made.

When he became tired, he sat down to rest. He wanted his mother near him, wanted her sitting close to him in the snowstorm, with no one else around. He didn't have to wait long for her because she had been on his trail. Never had he seen her so angry, so out of breath, and so covered with snow.

Sitting on the steps and looking at the car, he wanted his mother with him now. The car was parked not far away and he wanted to find the keys to the car and drive it away with his mother sitting next to him. He wanted to take her away somewhere so that they could go out to eat hamburgers and then get married and never come back. He wondered where the keys were. He worried about paying for the hamburgers because he didn't have any money. Worse still, he didn't know how to drive.

Waking with a start and sitting up in bed, he felt frightened as he remembered the dream he'd just had. In the dream, he was a lion, a strong and powerful lion. His father was a hunter looking for him. As a lion, he'd crept through the jungle quietly until he was within 10 feet of his father's back. He could see his father's shoulders and the back of his head. Leaping at his father, he roared a lion's roar and extended his sharp claws. Abruptly, he woke up, feeling cold and afraid.

He woke one summer morning, certain he'd be a scientist when he grew up. Putting his clothes on, he rapidly finished his breakfast. Then he dashed outside and ran down the block to tell his friend about science. His friend was home and the two of them found some empty bottles. As scientists, they carried their bottles around the neighborhood, picking up bugs and putting them into the bottles. By midmorning, their bottles were alive with a crawling mass of insects. When his father came home late in the afternoon, the boy proudly showed him a bottle half filled with dead or dying bugs.

A week after his ninth birthday, he tried to make a quart of nitroglycerine. Mixing the acid with the glycerine, he stirred the liquid with one of his mother's spoons, which turned black. The mixture wouldn't mix. He wondered if he ought to boil it on the stove in the kitchen. Finally, he poured the stuff on a bush, which eventually died. He told some of his friends about the experiment, but he threw the spoon away and never told his parents what he'd done.

By the time he was ten years old, he knew how babies came to be. He thought the whole matter of sex was preposterous. During the summer, he and his friends threw dirt clods at girls once in a while, to scare them away. When winter came, he and his cohorts threw snowballs at them. Sometimes, at night when he was getting ready for bed, he would look at his penis, shake his head, and say, "Never."

On the day he was twelve years old, he had a thought that lasted for three seconds. He was standing alone in center field, watching the pitcher and waiting for the batter to do something. He was bored because neither one of them was moving. The thought came but left in a flash. The thought was about a girl he knew. He wondered what it would be like to touch her softly on the face.

When he was sixteen, he touched her on the face and on her bare shoulders. He thought about touching her in some other places, too, but there were too many people around. She was beautiful, he thought, but he wondered what the other people thought about her. The other people didn't seem to notice. They were busy swimming. He wondered how he looked to her and he wished he had bigger muscles but he was glad he didn't look as flabby as his father did.

After graduating from high school, he found a job just for the summer. It wasn't much of a job, but it brought in some money. He saved some of the money for school, which would resume in the fall, but he didn't want to go to school any more. He was tired of school, tired of his home, bored with his summer job. Sometimes he wanted very much to get married, but most of the time he thought about going away somewhere, away from his girl and from his family. If he left, he wouldn't have to go to any more schools. He wondered if he could get a job on a ship. He wondered what New Zealand was like. He wondered about living in Rangoon and Oslo.

If the new person survives infancy, he moves into the second stage of development, called early childhood.

The stage of early childhood, or the anal period (as it is sometimes called), covers the second and third years of life. The child, building on a previously developed sense of trust, begins to assert himself. He typically becomes insistent about the idea that he can make his own decisions such as sleeping or not sleeping, eating or not eating, answering mother's call or not. As his physical ability increases, he normally develops an increasing independence, which may often be interpreted as rebellion by the parents.

A totally independent child, free of all restrictions, is something of a savage. Families rarely are able to tolerate a savage in their midst, so the child (no matter how delightfully savage he may be) is subject to a civilizing process. His independence may be curtailed; and if the parents believe he is simply rebellious rather than seeking autonomy, they may strongly oppose at least some of his activities. The parents may demand changes in the child's behavior. One of the changes involves control of bladder and bowel.

Infants do not have bladder and bowel control, so diapers are used to take care of the problem. By about the eighteenth month, a child normally has developed the neurological pathways that control bowel movement and he can be trained to exercise that control. Bladder control during the daytime usually takes a bit longer, but is usually well established by the end of the second year of life. Nighttime control (while sleeping) generally does not come until the child is about 3 years old. The child who is sometimes dirty, messy, and nonconforming is one who was probably able to achieve toilet training without feelings of shame and doubt about himself. The child who is always neat, orderly, and on time is probably overly responsible and overly controlled.

While there may be a neurological base for bowel and bladder control, one or both parents usually work with the child to help him establish that control. The civilizing process called toilet training is a minor landmark in the history of each individual. How the toilet training is accomplished and the way in which it is handled by parents and child may have an influence on behavior that is not at all related directly to toilet activities.

Although this later behavior indicates what may be a resolution of toilet training, it is greatly rewarded in our society. Being on time for class or for a date is considered a great virtue. Parents are very pleased when children conform to their wishes, and so are many teachers.

The life of the overly controlled person is not easy because many disturbances of routine and orderliness can cause a sense of unease, a feeling of anxiety.

The developmental task of early childhood is to form a sense of autonomy. Autonomy involves self-acceptance and some strivings toward personal independence.

In moving toward independence, the child tries out and experiments with independence from mother. It is a social achievement to be able to let mother go and trust her to return. Independence from father is also a social achievement.

During this period, the child optimally should come to feel he is an accepted human being, self-reliant but nevertheless able to use the help and guidance of his parents. To help him achieve this feeling of support and guidance, parents should be consistent both in what they allow and what they forbid.

The child should not be allowed to control the family; yet his struggle for autonomy must be accepted and encouraged so that he will learn to be independent.

■ If the parents ridicule the child, he will doubt himself and his autonomy.

TRUE   (TURN TO PAGE 29.)

FALSE   (TURN TO PAGE 33.)

During the fourth, fifth, and sixth years of life, the child's world expands. In the beginning, he had only one environment: home and mother. Now, however, he adds another environment to life: the neighborhood. His activities cover more territory and more people. In time, during these years of expansion, the child moves into a third environment: school.

As the child's activities expand, as he comes in contact with more and more people, he typically begins to develop an increasingly certain idea of who he is.

Little boys become aware that being a boy is different from being a girl and vice versa. The child's curiosity about his genitals and about differences in sexual roles reaches a peak. The natural outcome is in the discovery of pleasure through masturbation and in the playing of masculine and feminine roles with the parents as models.

■ If you believe masturbation is predictable and normal behavior, TURN TO PAGE 30.

■ If you believe masturbation is abnormal or dangerous to health, TURN TO PAGE 34.

During the fourth, fifth, and sixth years of life, the child begins to develop an increasingly certain idea of who he is, who mother is, and who father is. Slowly, at first, and then with more and more gusto, the boy competes with his father for the mother's attention and affection. The boy may daydream about running away with his mother to some private place they can call their own. Many boys have daydreams about doing away with father so that they can have mother all to themselves. Girls will often think about father the way that boys will think about mother. Girls may have daydreams about getting rid of mother.

During the ages of 4, 5, and 6, the child develops common and normal romantic feelings toward the parent of the opposite sex. At the same time, he will have feelings of rivalry and aggression toward the parent of the same sex.

■ Many children will not really recover from the feelings that develop during the years of 4, 5, and 6. (TURN TO PAGE 31.)

■ The feeling for mother and the feelings about father that develop during the years 4, 5, and 6 are passed by as the child gets older. What happens during those years is a temporary phase. (TURN TO PAGE 35.)

If the daydreams and hopes of the boy who is 4, 5, and 6 are fulfilled, trouble and turmoil develop.

If these dreams and hopes came true, the boy would be without a father; and he would be romantically involved with his own mother.

In order that the daydreams and hopes do not come true, the boy can develop what is sometimes called self-defeating behavior. He can learn how to defeat himself, how not to be successful, and how "to lose." A person can be motivated to lose if winning would cause too much trouble.

■ Self-defeating behavior is interesting, dramatic, but rarely found in adults. (TURN TO PAGE 32.)

■ Self-defeating behavior is common, widespread, and often seen in adult behavior. (TURN TO PAGE 36.)

In general, the third stage of development comes gradually to a close when the boy begins to see his father as someone he would like to be, eventually. The little girl might say, "If you can't beat them, join them," as she starts to see in her mother the sort of person she would someday like to be. The little girl gives up father and the little boy gives up mother as love objects.

The girl generally identifies with and copies the behavior of her mother. She decides to find her own man by learning to be a woman.

If the boy decides to learn how to be a man, he will, in a general way, identify with and copy the behavior of his father.

If the child does not identify, at least to some extent, with the parent of the same sex, he may have some difficulties as a grown-up person. For instance, if a girl identifies closely with her father, she may be so masculine when she is an adult that most men will be frightened away from her. She may, however, find a man who has in his youth identified with his mother. The result is a pairing off of a mannish female and a feminine man. This sort of pairing, which involves sexual role reversal, is not rare.

During the third stage of development, boys and girls have strong romantic and sexual feelings as well as feelings of rivalry and aggression about their parents. As the boy and girl move into the fourth stage of development (ages 7 through 11), those feelings become hidden under the surface. They are not expressed in behavior. They become latent. And so the fourth stage of development is called the latent period, the period during which many feelings are not expressed in behavior.

Everyone has feelings. People experience, as they move through their lives, a wide range of feelings and emotions. We cannot, however, see feelings or observe emotions. We see and observe behavior, and then we assume or guess about the feelings and emotions inside the observed person.

If feelings and emotions are expressed by some kind of observable behavior, they are said to be manifested.

Feelings and emotions that a person has, but that are not expressed in some kind of behavior, are called latent feelings, latent emotions.

■ During the latent period, boys and girls are no longer interested in or curious about sex.

AGREE   (TURN TO PAGE 37.)

DISAGREE   (TURN TO PAGE 40.)

During the last part of stage three and throughout all of stage four of development, the child's conscience expands. He begins to become aware of more rules, more subtle rules, more complicated rules, of behavior. A person's conscience does not begin at this time (it really begins much earlier in life), but it becomes enlarged and more adultlike during the fourth stage of development.

A person's conscience can be viewed as having two main parts. One part is filled with rules and regulations that say "Don't." The other part says "Do." In a way, then, a conscience is made up of inhibitions and ambitions.

■ During this stage of development, the boy will continue to try to identify with his father and the girl will try to identify with her mother. If the parent of the same sex does not have adequate or workable moral standards, the child will not develop workable or adequate moral standards. The child's conscience will be under-developed.

AGREE   (SEE PAGE 38.)

DISAGREE   (SEE PAGE 41.)

Each person moves along a time line that begins at the moment of conception and ends at death. Along the way, he evolves and changes.

As he moves from a microscopic being to a fully visible, physically mature adult, he passes through the fifth stage of development, which is called adolescence.

The beginning of adolescence cannot be sharply defined. Adolescence is a time of biological change, but from the moment of conception onward, people go through many biological changes. What makes adolescence a special time, and what sets it apart from the other stages of development, is the emergence of secondary sex characteristics.

Both boys and girls begin, normally, to have a more conscious awareness of their own sexual feelings and desires. An adolescent is very conscious of the changes in his body. Rapid growth increase and size change frequently cause clumsiness and poor coordination. Adjustment to the development of secondary sex characteristics is embarrassing. The newly surging sexual feelings create considerable conflict and are frequently a source of distress to the adolescent.

Sensitivity toward self is accompanied by an increased sensitivity toward the people around him. He is overly critical of adult attitudes, and his self-consciousness leads him to read personal meanings into statements where none were intended. This is often aggravated by comments from adults that indicate intolerance or amusement.

The adolescent years are problem years in nations that can afford to let people go through this fifth stage of development. Not all countries can afford to have adolescent people. In poor countries and in underdeveloped parts of the world, there may be no such thing as an adolescent.

Normally, adolescents are not productive. They are consumers—users, takers of things—rather than makers—builders and givers. In some nations of the world, children can (and usually must) go to school until they are nearly adults. These are the nations that have adolescent citizens. In other countries, children work, and they continue to work as they move through the biological changes toward adulthood. These countries need workers, not adolescent citizens. In poor countries, a person becomes a working adult rapidly.

If a nation is rich enough to be able to afford adolescent citizens, it is likely to have something called a generation gap.

The gap between the younger and the older generation is not inevitable. In the past, when the world moved at a slower pace, the child learned his father's trade. When that child grew up, he taught his own son the same trade. The work skills were passed from one generation to the next, and families were identified by the work they did. This identification is apparent in the last names of people. Most people named Smith will have a line of ancestors who were blacksmiths. Someone called Currier has forefathers who curried horses. The family history behind such names as Carpenter and Mason is obvious. Do you know anyone named William Computerprogrammer? What about Alice Jetpilot or Sandra Televisioncameraman?

The generation gap may not be inevitable, but it becomes predictable when the environment within which people live changes rapidly.

The major developmental task of the adolescent involves building a sense of personal identity.

Typically, the adolescent will grow away from his parents to become less and less a child and more and more an adult. The adolescent must go beyond his own family into a world that is more his own than his parents' world. He must, if he is to become an adult, gradually build a life for himself.

In a very general way, children believe adults are powerful. Children often have the idea that adults do what they want to do and that adults can manage and control their own affairs with ease. As children evolve into adolescence, they usually discover that adults are neither all powerful nor so highly skilled in the art of living. Such a discovery can cause the adolescent to think (and sometimes say), "Your way doesn't work very well. I'm going to do things *my* way." A comment such as that can lead to behavior that can develop an increased sense of personal identity on the part of the adolescent, especially if the young person is successful in what he does. A comment such as that, however, can also be interpreted by the parent as inappropriately rebellious behavior.

■ The comment quoted above can be viewed as a step toward independence and the development of a sense of identity. It can also be viewed as rebellion. Which view do you have:

It is a rebellious statement.   (SEE PAGE 39.)

It is a matter of identity.   (SEE PAGE 42.)

There are many parents who need to be parents. There are people whose lives are satisfying and happy if they have and rear children. Some of these people will resent the fact that their children mature and move away. It can be, for them, as though their purpose in life has been taken from them. These people may behave in ways that are designed to keep the adolescent at home forever.

If (A) the adolescent member of a family strives for increasing independence and works at the development of a sense of personal identity,

and (B) one or both parents resent the movement toward freedom,

then a contest will result.

The contest between parent and adolescent can end if the adolescent gives in and remains an adolescent for the rest of his life. The contest can also end if the adolescent develops a firm enough sense of identity to move into the adult years. This, of course, may mean a real breaking away from the parents. It does not mean that the contests will rage and explode around the house. Nor does it mean there will be open warfare or deadly rivalries between parents and the adolescent. It does mean, however, that the contests between the parents and the adolescent can be frequent and can take many forms.

You are ready to begin Chapter 3, page 43.

True! This leads back to the development of the self. Ridicule is definitely negative reflected appraisal, and the child sees himself as "bad" and unworthy of love.

When adults use force or threats of withdrawal of love to gain control over the child, they are severely threatening that child's autonomy or sense of being an adequate, independent person.

As an adult, this person may react to his lack of autonomy by timid conformity to others, or he may belligerently reject all authority figures.

GO DIRECTLY TO PAGE 21.

Correct. Masturbation is normal in children. Some psychiatrists and some psychologists believe that masturbation by adults is also normal and nonharmful.

It seems safe to predict that most (if not all) children will masturbate. Often, if problems arise, they are based not so much on the masturbatory activity as on the ways in which parents respond to it and the ways in which they handle the child.

PROCEED TO PAGE 22.

Correct. The feelings a child has during the years 4, 5, and 6 can stay with him for the rest of his life. Occasionally, the feeling will continue to center on the real mother and the real father. Most often, however, these feelings are apt to be transferred out of the world of childhood into the adult world. Then the feelings can become complicated and, often, can cause self-defeating behavior.

NOTE: This stage of behavior does gradually come to an end, at least in terms of the person's observable actions. There is a shift in behavior, a change, a modification in the way the child functions with both parents. There is a gradual and evolutionary shift from a lively to a more quiet and sedate style of life.

For now, turn to page 23.

You are wrong on two counts out of three.

Self-defeating behavior *is* interesting.

Self-defeating behavior *is not* necessarily dramatic. It can operate in quite and often unnoticed ways.

Self-defeating behavior *is* very frequently seen in adults.

START OVER ON PAGE 23.

Perhaps you were thinking that ridicule would not affect autonomy if it were a one-time thing, and that is correct. Children can tolerate lots of stress and frustration if they receive love and support most of the time.

Generally, though, ridicule is perceived by the child as rejection and negative reflected appraisal. Thus, he can feel much doubt about his own abilities and he can become hesitant to make decisions since they might lead to further rejection.

This child who is ridiculed may be dependent on others in adult life.

Return to page 20 and select the other answer.

Wrong. Masturbation is not abnormal, particularly among children. It is not harmful to health, although there are myths and old wives tales about its dangers. At one time, many people believed masturbation was responsible for some forms of blindness, deafness, baldness, insanity, and pimples. It is not.

START OVER ON PAGE 21.

Wrong. What happens during these years is a temporary phase for a few people, but many children will carry the feelings into adulthood. The feelings about mother and father may be shifted from them to other people. In other words, the feelings can remain, but the targets of those feelings can change.

TRY AGAIN ON PAGE 22.

Correct. Self-defeating behavior is common, widespread, and often seen in the behavior of adults. The implications of this sort of behavior are discussed in Section II. For now, you may learn a little about self-defeating behavior by reading the three examples that follow:

1. Fred was obviously smart. He did very well in high school and during the first 3 years of college. In his senior year, however, his grades began going down. Eventually he flunked out. His parents were mystified, hurt, and angry. Fred was not in trouble with a girl, or in debt, or involved in protests and riots, or on drugs. When asked why, he merely shrugged his shoulders.

2. Pat had saved money for 2 years. She bought some new clothes, a good set of luggage, and made reservations at good hotels. She bought a round-trip plane ticket that allowed her to spend a month in Europe. When she was standing in line at Kennedy International, she realized she didn't have a passport.

3. Jim had wanted a date with Susan for a long time. Finally she agreed to go out with him. On the way to pick her up, he ran out of gas.

CONTINUE ON TO PAGE 24.

Wrong. Boys and girls remain curious about and interested in sex. They may not show this in a way that is obvious and similar to what they may have shown at an earlier age, but they are still curious and still interested.

Turn to page 40 for the correct answer.

Wrong. Yes, the parents are important. Yes, the boy will identify with father and the girl will identify with mother. Yes, the moral standards that mothers and fathers have are important to the child who is traveling through stage four of development. But other people and their standards are important too.

If the moral standards of the parents are not workable, if they are not adequate for the child, that child may get some help in the development of conscience from teachers, from other adults, and from members of the gang in which he is a member.

During the fourth stage of development, the child moves into a series of experiences in which he is more on his own. Boys and girls experience life with a gang of near equals. The rules and regulations as well as the goals and interests of the gang may be of great help in the development of conscience.

START OVER ON PAGE 25.

There are two potential parent-child relationships that lead to impulsive, rebellious behavior.

One is growing up in an atmosphere where there is no self-control on the part of the parents. The parents are impulsive and rebellious to society, showing a disregard for law and order, and living a life of self-gratification. A child reared under these conditions will probably identify with his parents and be rebellious even toward them.

The other relationship exists when parents cater to the whims and demands of the child and try to appease him while at the same time pushing him to achieve and perform. Giving in to him really serves to increase his demands. Pushing and nagging only encourage his resistance. From the parental attitude of oversubmission, the adolescent's own attitude becomes one of oversubmission to his impulses and desires.

Placing the adolescent under a burden of gratitude and a sense of duty also encourages impulsiveness and rebellion.

If the comment on the previous page was said in the sort of settings described above, the chances are it could have been a rebellious comment.

How can you, the individual, keep in mind that if you are to diagnose the meaning behind comments people make it is often useful to know the setting or the environment in which the comments were made. The statement "I'm going to do things *my* way" can be interpreted and diagnosed with some accuracy if you have more information than you were given on page 27.

TURN TO PAGE 28.

Correct. The child is still curious about sex. The boy may play "doctor" games and examine girls, but there are times when he may prefer to examine boys.

Most relationships will be with other children of the same sex. A girl will play with girls, often in a small gang. Gangs of boys commonly exist because boys will prefer to play with other boys.

In some ways, the fourth stage of development is a homosexual stage. It has been referred to as a period of normal homosexuality.

Almost all people are a mixture of what is feminine and what is masculine. There is no firm dividing line between the two. To extend that idea a little further: It is possible that most human beings, especially by the time they are grown up, are a mixture of heterosexual and homosexual factors.

TURN TO PAGE 25.

Do you disagree? You are right if you do.

By the time a child moves through the fourth stage of development (ages 7 through 11), his parents have become less important to him than before. In addition to his parents, the child has the gang. It is typical and normal for him to belong to some kind of gang or group of peers (Brownies, Cub Scouts, Indian Guides, Blue Birds, etc.) during the fourth stage. He can get nonparental guidance from the group and this will help in the development of conscience.

During the years from about age 7 to 11, a best friend is important. Also, children within this age group are usually concerned about their popularity with the other children. Reputation is a worrisome factor in this fourth stage of development.

During this stage, the child may have great surges of feelings (sometimes called "crushes") about some teacher, about television personalities, about older children of the same sex, and about sports heroes and movie stars. If the child likes to read books, he may become swept away in the stories and his feelings may rise and fall as the characters in the book succeed or fail in their adventures. He comes alive, part of the time, through the lives and experiences of other people. By forming even a temporary bond with some kind of hero or star, the boy or girl can develop a somewhat better level of self-esteem.

GO TO PAGE 26.

In a way you are wrong. You were not given enough information to go on.

NOTE: Living conditions have changed drastically and dramatically within recent years. The parents of today's adolescent citizens can remember a world without television. Some might even recall that, at one time, all airplanes had propellers and most cars were painted black. These were the days before nylon, cellophane tape, and ballpoint pens.

The parents of today's adolescents grew up during the Depression of the 1930's, during World War II and the beginnings of the Cold War. The world was different then; the environment in which they lived was different. Living conditions were not the same as they are today.

The adolescents of today were born into and have experienced a world that is vastly different from the world their parents once knew. The difference is great enough to foster different views and values and ideals, and these differences lead to a gap between generations.

Turn to page 39 for the more correct answer.

3

ADULTHOOD

By the time he was twenty-one, he was finished with school. He had a job but he couldn't decide whether to get married or move to New Zealand.

***

When he was twenty-five, he wrote a letter to his father. In the letter, he said he could name the two biggest surprises of his life. One: He was surprised that babies could be so messy and smell so bad. Two: He was surprised to find out how much his wife knew about him now. In the letter to his father, he also mentioned saving money so he could take his wife and his children to New Zealand with him.

***

By the eighth year of his marriage he began to think about running away. He'd been saving money for the trip to New Zealand for five years, but sometimes he wondered if he'd ever get there. At night, he dreamed about going, and in the early morning he told his wife about the dreams. She made love with him then. At breakfast she asked him if he would like to go to New Zealand by himself; there was money enough for that. He told her he couldn't go without her.

***

He gave his son a small chemistry set for a birthday present. The next day an old memory came to mind and he began to worry a little. He wondered if his son would try to make nitroglycerine.

***

He dreamed a long dream the night before his son graduated. In the dream he was walking somewhere, surrounded by a strange kind of mist and soft light. He didn't know if it was dawn or sunset, but he knew he was alone in a place he'd never seen before. No, he wasn't alone. Far ahead, he could see an old man walking through the mist. The man was walking away from him; he could not see the man's face but he knew it was his father. He tried to run, to catch up, to walk alongside his father. He couldn't run. He tried but he could only walk. He looked behind. He saw a young man walking far behind and he wanted to stop, to wait for the young man who was his son. He couldn't stop himself from walking, though, and he knew he was caught halfway between his father and his son, walking somewhere in the middle of time.

He looked at his birthday cake and he was awed by the fifty candles. Half a century, he thought as he looked through the shimmering air heated by the fifty small flames. From across the table, his wife smiled at him and his son held up a daughter so she could see all the candles. Her young eyes were opened wide with surprise, and when the fifty-year-old man saw her, he laughed with affection and with a deepening sense of the meaning of time.

He wondered what he would do after next year. He wondered what he would do when he couldn't go to work any more. He didn't want to retire. He thought about going to New Zealand and then he remembered that wasn't possible now.

He was sixty-eight years old when they operated on his prostate. They gave him a spinal anesthetic and he watched as they probed and snipped and cauterized him. They all seemed so young, especially the nurses, and they all moved so fast. After the operation, he felt very old and tired for a month, but then he started going for walks and he began to feel better.

When he was seventy years old, his son gave a birthday party for him. His wife went with him and they held each other's hand as the cake was brought in, and everyone sang the birthday song. He blew out the candles with two breaths and then he looked around the room at the people there. His son was gray haired now and his granddaughter held her baby (his great grandson) in her arms. Everything was fine, he thought. Everyone was getting along all right, better than he had hoped, and he felt within himself a serene sense of completeness. He kissed his wife lightly and wondered which one of them would live on, alone. He felt at peace, even with that thought on his mind.

He didn't cry when his wife died, but he felt alone and lost and cold to the center of his bones. He didn't cry. He didn't want to. He went home after the funeral and quietly sat down in his old chair and looked at their wedding picture for a long time.

He couldn't sleep. He was tired, but he couldn't sleep so he turned the light on and sat up in bed. He put his glasses on, opened a book, and began to read. He read two pages before his mind began to wander. He put the book down, took off his glasses, and turned out the light. He lay back down on the bed and dozed, dreaming again about his wife and their young children and the money they were saving for the trip to New Zealand. He was dreaming of a seashore there when he died at the age of seventy-two.

If the person somehow survives the adolescent years, he moves into the sixth stage of development.

The sixth stage is called early adulthood. It includes a 15-year span of time covering the years from 21 through 35.

Several important events can take place during early adulthood. One of these events is marriage, although many people get married before this stage of development. Another important event is having children. Most people who have children have them during early adulthood.

Probably the most important event during early adulthood is the development of intimacy with another or with a few other people.

People can achieve some intimacy by being with each other as they experience different activities. People can achieve intimacy by skiing together, by eating at the same table, by watching movies, football games, and television together, and by going to school together. When people experience activities together, some intimacy results. The intimacy, however, may be superficial unless people experience each other.

When people experience activities together, they may only be sharing the time and the space their bodies take up. Sharing time and space is superficial compared with sharing ideas, thoughts, opinions, beliefs, feelings, and attitudes.

Real intimacy involves sharing oneself with another person.

■ Intimacy means having a genuine and deeply personal heterosexual relationship.

AGREE   (SEE PAGE 53.)

DISAGREE   (SEE PAGE 56.)

Many young adults have to find a job and go to work. If a person works for 5 or 10 years or more, he usually has a series of jobs. Sometimes, people will have a series of loosely related jobs either in the same organization or in several different organizations.

A series of jobs can be called a career. A career is a general line of work a person follows.

In a general way, people end up in one career or another because of their backgrounds and because of the experiences they have had in living. And, while a career may say something about what an individual does on a job, the career a person has tells something about him as an individual. The kind of career a person has, and his behavior while working, may reveal some of that person's childhood experience.

The kind of career a person has can tell something about that person's childhood experiences. How a person behaves while working can reveal something about his experiences while growing up. For example, it is possible to speculate that really successful accountants find satisfaction in turning out work that is well organized and precise. They may place a high value on orderliness and neatness. Perhaps you can look back in this book and reread what was said about toilet training. There may be a connection between some successful accountants and the kind of toilet training they experienced.

Most people who have jobs have supervisors. There are, of course, adequate and inadequate supervisors in any organization. Generally, though, the way individuals feel about the supervisor and the manner in which they respond to him are apt to resemble the responses they made to parents and to other adults during childhood.

There may be some relationships between the experiences a person has while growing up and the career he eventually chooses. There may also be connections and relationships between the first family and the second family in which a person lives.

When a person is growing up, he lives in the first family of his life. When he marries, he lives in the second family of his life.

If the young adult decides to marry, the quality of his marriage may be based on the quality of the marriage of his parents. The quality of life in the second family is often based on the quality of life in the first family.

■ Marriage can exacerbate problems. That is, marriage can bring out problems or feelings in a person that otherwise would have remained latent or dormant if he had stayed single.

TRUE   (TURN TO PAGE 54.)

FALSE   (TURN TO PAGE 58.)

In the search for intimate relationships, the young adult is influenced by all his past relationships. His feelings of affection and closeness may be based on: (a) love or affectional relationships he has had throughout his life so far, including perhaps even the primal dialogue; (b) how he feels about himself and how much he knows about himself.

If the young adult decides to marry, he may have more opportunities for a variety of intimate relationships than a person who remains single. Not only does a married person have a spouse, but often there are children with whom he may have intimate relationships.

The achievement of intimacy between a parent and a child may sometimes (but not always) be a fine and productive experience for the growing child. However, there may be times when a child is robbed of childhood by a parent who expects the child to act and think as an adult. Also, it may be difficult to develop an equality of intimacy between the parent and the child. They are not equal; they are not peers.

Intimacy, a durable and mature sort of intimacy, can be achieved between people who are reasonably equal to each other. Overall, though, close relationships with peers are more difficult to establish than close relationships with people who are in a subordinate or superior position. Sometimes one or both parents will try to develop intimacy with their children either because they are unable to do so with each other or because they (the parents) choose to avoid the development of mutual intimacy.

Middle age begins at the middle of a person's possible life-span.

In the United States and Canada, and in a few other countries, people can expect to live to be about 70 years old. Middle age starts at the midpoint, beginning at age 35 and ending at age 65. This is the seventh stage of development.

In a general sense, people who can deal successfully with the relevant factors of middle age have already experienced at least two successful achievements in living. They have already formed a generally adequate sense of their own identity and they have achieved a reasonably satisfying level of durable intimacy with one or a few other people.

Middle-aged adults are usually not tolerant of the younger generation. The point should be made, also, that the younger generation is usually not tolerant of the middle-aged adult.

The lack of tolerance middle-aged people feel when they view the younger generation may sometimes be obvious. At other times, however, it may be well disguised. Eventually, though, the lack of tolerance may be based on a simple factor that has wide-reaching effects. This simple factor is the matter of differences between people.

People usually feel most comfortable when they can associate, at least superficially, with people who are much like themselves. They usually feel ill at ease when they are required to deal with others who are different from them. Today's younger generation is different from those who now are in middle age. Each is in a position to be intolerant of the other group.

The developmental task of middle age is sometimes called generativity. *Generativity* refers to middle age behavior that fosters and promotes the development of the younger generation.

If an adult has achieved a sense of identity and formed intimate relationships, he can expand his life and find further satisfaction by helping the younger generation to become genuinely grown up. This means, in many instances, simply allowing young people to assume the responsibilities and the rights that are theirs. In other instances, it can mean gently pushing the younger generation to do what they are supposed to do.

Generativity connotes all aspects of responsible parenthood.

■ Only parents can achieve aspects of true generativity.

YES   (TURN TO PAGE 55.)

NO   (TURN TO PAGE 59.)

The eighth stage of personality development is the last one. The eighth stage of development is called old age. It covers the years from age 65 to the end of life.

During the old age years, most people think about the lives they have lived. They usually try to decide whether they have had a good life or not, according to some standard of good and bad.

During the old age years, the person must adjust to physical degeneration. He must deal with the feelings and the realities that come to the front as every organ and system of the body slowly falls apart. He must face the prospect of dying.

■ Which man is the more typical:

Jack resents getting old, and to him, death is the ultimate insult of all time. (SEE PAGE 60.)

John accepts his deterioration and believes death will bring rewards in the next life. (SEE PAGE 62.)

During the old age years, most people think about the lives they have lived. Most old people spend time combing through the years, reflecting about how life has gone for them, and working at the developmental task of old age: achievement of a sense of completeness or integrity.

A sense of completeness or integrity seems necessary and appropriate in old age because there is a review of one's life, a wrapping-up, or an effort at fading from the scene with a sense of having done one's best or at least of having tried. In spite of a decline in health and abilities, old age can be a time of peace and contentment.

In general, the achievement of completeness or integrity is based on the level of the previously developed sense of personal identity. The greater the degree of a sense of identity, the greater will be the degree of a sense of completeness.

In old age, people review their lives and think about what they have done and what they have not done so that when they die someone can write an obituary about them for the newspaper. The obituary will describe some of the things they have done, but it will rarely describe the things they have not done.

As an individual who is not yet 65 years of age or older, write your obituary on a blank sheet of paper. You should try to be factual as you describe what you have done up to the present moment. Beyond that point, you can use your imagination.

Funerals are older than man's written history. They existed before Christ, before Moses, and before the first tribal chieftains of China roamed the plains of that ancient land.

The ritual of a funeral is, in some places, a time for music and dancing. In other places, funerals are meant to be times of mourning and grief. Whether they are joyful or sad, funerals are designed for the living.

In our time and in our society, the funeral is a ritual that can relieve feelings of anger, guilt, or loss on the part of those who still live. Funerals can be an emotional experience that helps the survivors deal with the death of someone close to them. Funerals are, in general, necessary.

Some funerals are poorly attended and are surrounded by an aura of distaste and repugnance. (For instance, think of Lee Harvey Oswald's funeral.) In contrast, some funerals are attended by thousands and are surrounded by an atmosphere of stately magnificence mixed with a profound sense of loss. (John F. Kennedy's funeral, of course, as well as Ghandi's and Martin Luther King's burials were internationally acknowledged.) If there had been no funeral ceremonies for these men, what might have happened to the emotions people had about these men?

Thinking about the death and burial of well-known people may help to understand the process of the death and burial of a parent or a very good friend or a spouse. Funerals dull the sense of loss and help mourning to run its course. They are necessary because they help the living to better handle the feelings they have about someone's death.

You have reached the end of Section I.

TURN TO PAGE 64.

Wrong. To agree with that last sentence is, in this case, incorrect.

A person can have an intimate relationship with another person; that other person can be called a very close friend. A very close friend can be male or female.

Perhaps, again, you thought of intimacy as sexual or only sexual. Intimacy may or may not include sexual activity.

It is possible for two people to have a sexual relationship and, at the same time, to have no real intimacy with each other.

Return to page 46 for another choice.

True is correct. Marriage can exacerbate negative and destructive feelings that otherwise would have remained dormant or latent. Marriage can also exacerbate feelings of affection and closeness, feelings of trust and sharing that were experienced at an earlier age.

It is often difficult to predict whether a marriage will arouse feelings that can become destructive or feelings that can lead to intimacy. You may need to keep in mind, though, that a reasonably good predictor of the quality of a young adult's marriage is the quality of the parents' marriage. If the parents achieved a good and stable level of intimacy in their marriage, the young adult may have a reasonably good chance for achieving the same thing in his own marriage. This is because he had good role models.

You are ready for page 48.

Wrong.

It is possible for almost all middle-aged people (not just middle-aged parents) to become involved in, and to gain great satisfaction by way of, generativity.

RETURN TO PAGE 49.

You disagree, and that is the right thing to do. Intimacy can be achieved with both males and females.

Intimacy can involve the sharing of one's own ideas, thoughts, opinions, beliefs, feelings, and attitudes with another person. Before such factors can be shared, they must be known. So, it seems as though the development of intimacy is based on a previously developed sense of personal identity.

It is usually not possible for a young adult to achieve intimacy unless a sense of identity has already developed. To be able to be intimate in a relationship indicates that both people who are involved have reasonably well-developed senses of personal identity.

In a very broad way, not only must individuals who are able to form intimate relationships know themselves, but also they must trust. Intimacy can involve trusting oneself and trusting the other person in the relationship. The young adult will usually be cautious at the beginning of a relationship. If the caution continues, intimacy is hindered and the cautious person may say, "Deep down, I don't really trust that other person." It could be more honest, however, for the person to say, "Maybe I don't trust myself."

Intimacy is not a specific, tightly knit facet of human behavior. It exists at different levels. At one extreme, there are some closed-up people who never share anything about themselves. At the other extreme there are some rare people who relate completely, who share themselves with great satisfaction.

Where do you fit?

On a blank page with circles arranged as shown below, fill in the names of eight people with whom you are most intimate. These are the persons with whom you really share yourself. Those persons closest to you (the middle circle) are the ones with whom you are most intimate; and those further away, the ones with whom you are less intimate.

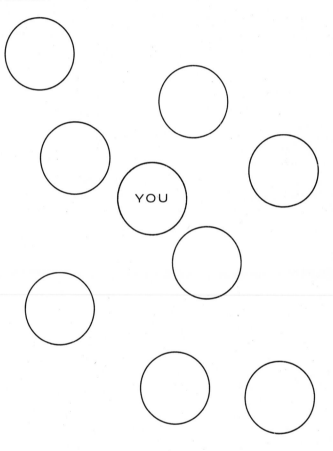

NOW TURN TO PAGE 47.

Wrong. Marriage can bring out many feelings that have been latent. Married people are sometimes surprised at the feelings that come to the surface in their marriage.

Marriage arouses all kinds of feelings, and this includes not only the negative but also the positive feelings that reside within the person.

Choose the other answer on page 47.

No is correct.

A middle-aged person does not need to be a parent in order to achieve the developmental task called generativity. Those who are parents may be generative in more obvious ways, but almost all middle-aged adults can find satisfaction in helping the young. Sometimes the helping involves not being obstructive or hindering to the younger generation.

Some middle-aged people have difficulty in dealing with generative tasks. They may be distracted from the tasks by concerns about their own place in the world and by the feelings and emotions that arise when their own parents grow old and die.

In a broad and general sense, middle-aged people must deal with the advancing younger generation, with their own aged parents, and with their own position in the overall scene.

■ People who are middle aged usually have a strong sense of time and the meaning of time. Usually, if they think about living, they can look to the future and see themselves on the decline and can look to the past and see missed opportunities. This, of course, implies that there are factors in middle age living that can cause the person to be depressed or angry.

AGREE   (TURN TO PAGE 61.)

DISAGREE (TURN TO PAGE 63.)

Correct.

Elderly people usually resent getting old, getting weak, getting sick. They may wonder, "Why me? I'm a decent person."

Nearly all people in our society fear death, even if they have strong religious beliefs. Children, especially at ages 4 or 5, fear death, partly because it is mysterious and partly because adults are usually serious when they talk about it. Throughout the other stages of life, people typically deny the possibility of death, and they may refuse to think about it for more than a few seconds at a time. A great many people may think about their own suicides; but often they think, concurrently, about how sorry people would be if they died. That is, they think about the result of death, rather than death itself.

For the person who is in old age, death is often seen as the ultimate insult. Fear of death is usually accompanied by anger that life should end before a person is really ready. If a person who is old has been ill and incapacitated, he may be more angry and resentful of death than if he had had good health until almost the end.

TURN TO PAGE 51.

In this case, to agree is correct.

There are factors in middle age living that can cause the middle-aged person to be depressed or angry. He can look into the future and see decline for himself. For some, the concerns about decline may center on the decline of physical abilities. Strength and stamina go down as the years pass. So do reflex speed, hearing ability, and sexual power. While desires and ambitions may remain the same, the ability to satisfy desires and achieve ambitions declines.

Middle-aged people can also look to their own past years with some sense of regret. They can wonder why they did not write that novel or take that trip or get more education. Some may even say quietly to themselves, "Well, I followed all the rules and I was a good person all the way, but I wish I'd had more fun."

While the years of middle age may bring feelings of anger and depression or feelings of regret, middle-aged people may be able to experience great satisfactions by way of generativity.

No matter how totally committed the person may be, the fact of being middle aged is inescapable. This may be especially the situation for people who are in the middle of middle age (from ages 45 to 55). A person in this age range is obviously no longer a young adult, but he is still far away from the usual age of retirement. He is in between ages, almost in the same sense an adolescent is in between. The adolescent is neither a child nor an adult. The middle-aged person is neither young nor ancient. He is, simply, middle aged. No matter how firmly he may become involved with generativity, he must still contend with decline and the usual feelings of regret over missed opportunities.

NOW GO TO PAGE 50.

Sorry, you are wrong.

John's acceptance of aging and death is not typical.

Religious beliefs may be comforting to the elderly person. The dying person may not feel very certain how he will die or what dying will be like. Uncertainty rarely brings a feeling of comfort.

Read about the more typical reaction on page 60.

Wrong.

There are many factors in middle age living that can bring about depressed or angry feelings.

Turn back to page 61 to read of only a few such factors.

4

BASIC
SOCIAL
RELATIONSHIPS

The two men woke an hour before dawn. They ate a cold breakfast, talking quietly and laughing softly in the manner of friends who had been together many times before. When they were finished eating, they picked up their rifles and clicked one round into the firing chamber and pressed four rounds into the magazine. Then they walked away from the camp and into the dark and silent forest. They walked quietly for a mile, through the trees and small clearings, before they came to a place where the ground slanted upward to a ridge. They could not see the crest of the ridge in the darkness, but they both knew that on the other side of the ridge there was a broad meadow covered with buffalo grass turned brown and yellow by the autumn cold.

The two men parted. One walked away to the north for two hundred yards and climbed carefully to the top of the ridge. He sat down on the ground and leaned back against a pine tree. He put the rifle in his lap and waited. He knew his friend was still walking south and that he would soon be climbing to his own position on the ridge a quarter of a mile away.

He waited. To the east, a thin gray strip of dawn began to show, and he could almost make out the broad meadow below him. He thought he could hear the elk grazing and chewing the buffalo grass, but he wasn't sure.

The edge of dawn had changed from gray to pink when the man aimed through his telescopic sight and fired. The great elk shuddered, leaped forward and fell to the ground as the rest of the herd ran swiftly to the south. The man heard the sound of his friend's rifle and saw another large elk fall in the meadow. The man felt pleased with his own marksmanship and he felt happy for his friend.

There are men who welcome the hunting season. Whether they are after ducks or deer, possum or elk, they enjoy the smell of oiled leather boots and they enjoy the heft of a rifle or shotgun. Most of all, it seems, they enjoy the company of other men.

There are men who prefer fishing, and they will fish with other men. Some prefer a poker game or a game of pool or golf; or, if they are wealthy, a chukker of polo. And in poker, pool, golf, and polo, the game usually calls for male companionship.

Women may not hunt or play polo, but you can find them getting together over coffee in the neighborhood, forming gardening clubs, organizing bridal showers and baby showers, and running parent teacher organizations.

Men often enjoy the company of other men. Women find satisfaction in socializing with other women. The enjoyment and the satisfaction are not entirely based on purely adult motivations. The behavior is related to an earlier period of life called the latency phase.

Usually there are strong relationships between adult behavior and childhood behavior. The latency behavior of going with a gang, of enjoying (and sometimes preferring) the company of people of the same sex, can be seen in adults.

During the latency period, boys generally prefer the companionship of other boys. Girls usually prefer to be with other girls. Such behavior does not disappear when the person moves out of the latent phase and moves into the adolescent and adult phases of life. Such behavior often remains and is often observable in adults.

Some men prefer the company and companionship of other men over and above any kind of relationship they may have with women. Some women would rather have only female friends and not have to bother at all with male friends. Most people, however, seem to enjoy having a mixture of friendships.

It usually seems typical for adolescents and adults to have both male and female friends.

■ Friends are people who are friendly to each other all the time.

YES   (SEE PAGE 69.)

NO   (SEE PAGE 72.)

There are people who have talent, beauty, skill, sophistication, knowledge, high intelligence, or priceless abilities who would rather not hear any sort of compliment. They are made uneasy by a positive comment. Even a slight element of praise may cause them to feel uncomfortable, perhaps slightly anxious. If, for instance, someone says to them, "You're really a fine person," they may smile, shrug a shoulder, and think to themselves, "you say that now, but wait until you get to know me."

There are men who work out with weights, who do sit-ups and push-ups by the dozen, who take vitamin pills and make certain they eat plenty of protein, and who somehow manage to spend a lot of time at the beach or by a pool building up a good tan. If a woman says to them, "You have a beautiful body," they may respond with, "Aw, my legs are too thin."

There are women who spend half a day getting ready for a date. The last 2 hours are spent putting on facial makeup with the precision and fine skill of an artist. When the man arrives, he may say, "You look beautiful," to which the woman might say, "Oh, but my eyes are bloodshot."

■ Which of the following seems to be more appropriate:

The quotations cited above are merely examples of polite modesty and everyone should behave that way. (TURN TO PAGE 70.)

The quotations indicate that some people may try to undo compliments. (TURN TO PAGE 73.)

Genuine friendships involve intimacy. Intimacy involves a sharing of self with another person or with a few other people. Intimacy includes a strong, mutual trust and a mutual respect. It also includes having a loving but not necessarily dependent attachment with another person. Intimacy, however, is not made up of sweetness and lyrical poems. Intimacy can often involve anxiety, particularly at the beginning of a relationship.

In order to develop an intimate relationship with another person, one must be willing to take the risk of being open about one's own ideas, thoughts, opinions, beliefs, feelings, and attitudes. You must risk exploring yourself. There is usually no such risk when you are called on to deal with an enemy.

It is sometimes more difficult and perhaps more anxiety-provoking to have a relationship with an intimate friend than with a person you can call an enemy.

Any relationship with an enemy may be carried on at a distance. There is little risk involved in a relationship with an enemy because the form and style of that relationship are more fixed and more certain than the relationship with a friend.

There are people who prefer to have enemies, to live at a distance from all others, probably because enemies, for them, are safer to deal with than friends. The individuals who would rather have enemies than friends may not appear hostile or antagonistic. Some may seem pleasant, polite, at least superficially at ease, but they may enjoy arguments and civilized debates about intellectual topics. They may barricade themselves behind the intellectual topics, and you may know with great certainty where they stand on topics such as politics, religion, family living; but you may know very little of their inner feelings about themselves, their attitudes, beliefs, and opinions.

On a blank sheet of paper, list three friends you have (or have had).

What did you learn about yourself from these people? How did these friendships increase your sense of personal identity? What price did you pay for these friendships? (price does not refer to money).

List two enemies you have (or have had).

What did you learn about yourself from these people?

What price would you have had to pay in order to have these people for enemies?

We each can have relationships with men and with women. We each can have relationships with friends and with enemies. Also, we can relate with people who have different status positions in relation to us.

There are three levels of status in human relationships:

1. Peer status: Peers are equals, colleagues, partners.

2. Superordinate status: Superordinates are people who rank above us in some way or other. The captain is the superordinate of the corporal; the teacher is the superordinate of the student, at least in elementary school.

3. Subordinate status: Subordinates are people who rank below us. Children are subordinates of parents, and an apprentice is a subordinate of the master craftsman.

■ In most circumstances, relations with a peer are more difficult than relations with either superordinates or subordinates.

AGREE (SEE PAGE 71.)

DISAGREE (SEE PAGE 74.)

Yes is incorrect.

If you think that friends are people who are friendly to each other all the time, you are wrong. Maybe you need to go back to Chapter 3 and read about the development of intimacy. Friends are rarely friendly all of the time. Genuine friendships go beyond the superficial, and there may be closeness and warmth mixed in periodically with distance and anger in a genuine friendship.

RETURN TO PAGE 65.

If you thought the quotations were simply indicators of polite modesty, you are wrong.

There are phrases we can all use when we think about human behavior. When someone ignores or turns away a compliment, we can say, "How modest," and let it go with that. Another handy phrase is, "He inherited that from his father." Still another is, "Well, people are that way naturally."

Such phrases and sayings may sometimes be useful and once in a while they may be accurate, but it is possible that they are just substitutes for thinking. To say that someone turns away a compliment because of modesty brings up the next question: "Why is the person modest?" Another phrase can be used then, such as, "No one likes to hear bragging." It is almost as though acknowledging a positive attribute about oneself is bad behavior.

START OVER ON PAGE 66.

If you agree, you are right.

Social relations with peers are more difficult than relations with either superordinates or subordinates, especially if intimacy is a factor in the relationship.

Freedom exists in relationships with peers. The freedom that comes with equality between two people is not philosophical. It is not some ideal stated in a charter; it is real and it must be dealt with if the relationship is to endure.

Under many circumstances, it appears as though an equality of relationships cannot often endure. It seems as though many people avoid equality, perhaps because in an equal relationship individuals must depend on themselves and on their personal resources and the sense of identity to keep the relationships going. It may be simpler or less difficult to turn an equal relationship into an unequal one or to start from the beginning of the relationship in a subordinate or superordinate position.

Early in life, the important superordinates for most people are called parents. There are, also, teachers, den mothers, scoutmasters, coaches, Blue Bird leaders, captains, and supervisors. Each of these individuals occupies a superordinate position with some measure of authority. People in authority positions exert control over the relationship, and that control governs the behavior of the superordinate and the subordinate. There is somewhat less freedom since the miniature social system decides much of the behavior. The individuals involved are not required to decide the nature of the relationship in all its aspects.

START CHAPTER 5, PAGE 75.

No is correct.

If you disagree with that last sentence, you are right.

Friends are not necessarily friendly all the time.

If you know someone whom you consider to be a friend and if that person is consistently agreeable and always pleasant, stop for a moment to consider the quality of the relationship.

If someone you know always agrees with your viewpoint and never questions or disagrees with what you say, that person is exactly the kind of person you are (is that possible?) or else the relationship is superficial. It may be comfortable and serene to know someone who never questions or disagrees with you, but is it honest?

In the formation of genuine friendships, the basic building blocks are the shared intimacies. The development of intimacy has already been mentioned in this book (page 67).

You are now ready for page 66.

Yes, some people may try to undo compliments. You are right.

While a sense of modesty may sometimes cause a person to turn away or undo a compliment, it may be that some other factors of behavior are operating. For example, the behavior may involve an avoidance of success. To avoid success a person may resort to self-defeating behavior.

A person may turn away or undo a compliment in an effort to avoid relationships that are too friendly. There are individuals who may avoid intimate relationships with others. They may say to themselves, "If that person really gets to know me, he won't like me anymore." (What can you say about a person's self-concept if he says that about himself?) It may be that some people prefer superficial relationships rather than genuine and intimate relationships. It may be that some few people would rather have enemies than friends.

NOW GO TO PAGE 67.

If, in this case, you disagree, you are incorrect.

Usually, peer relationships are more difficult than relationships with superordinates or subordinates.

Return to page 68 and try again.

5

SEXUAL RELATIONSHIPS

From the beginning she knew she would be chosen. She knew they would pick her out of the group, give her specialized training, and send her on the mission because she was a woman. Women had more stamina, they said, and women could endure more pain and survive greater loneliness than men.

Now that she was finished with all the training and because the technicians and specialists had done their jobs well, there was little for her to do on the long journey. When she reached her destination, she would be busy, but the trip, she concluded, was a bore. Two of the specialists had told her to keep herself occupied and so she used up time reading books from the microfilmed library and speaking into the tape recorder.

She had talked into the microphone an hour a day for the first week. During the second and third weeks, she felt compelled to speak more and more often until now, in the seventh week of her journey, she recorded her own voice for more than six hours out of every twenty-four. Most of the time she talked about the people she had known. Sometimes she described the men she disliked, but more often she spoke of the men she had loved. Once in a while she sang into the microphone. When she did that, she pretended she was singing softly to Charles or to Bob.

When she was not reading or talking or singing, she ate slowly or busied herself with the switches and levels and dials on the equipment that surrounded her. When she could think of nothing else to do, she looked out the windows of the space capsule. Earth had long ago disappeared from view in the black and endless void of space and, at this distance, earth's sun was merely another star.

She glanced at one of the dials and saw she was hundred million miles beyond the edge of the solar system. She smiled and began to hum and then to sing. It was a quiet song for Charles.

If you have read the story about Robinson Crusoe, perhaps you can recall the time he went mad. He had been on the island, alone, for a number of years. The lack of companionship, so he says in the book, took its toll and he put his head down and cried and then he ran wildly through the jungle and along the windy beaches, screaming and shooting his musket. He did not become a quiet man again until he was exhausted.

Crusoe's story is fictional, but there are many factual reports of people who slide away from reality after a period of isolation from other humans. Prisoners in solitary confinement often experience a deterioration in their own mental functioning. Volunteers who are research subjects in sensory deprivation (in which light, sound, heat, cold, and some of the force of gravity as well as the company of other people are removed from the environment) will often feel strange feelings and sometimes hallucinate in the same way a person with a mental illness might. Research scientists who work in the fields of space medicine and space psychology are concerned about the effects a long voyage may have on an astronaut. Such a trip might take 2 or 3 years. If the capsule contained only one astronaut, would she be able to keep herself intact and reasonably well adjusted? No one knows yet.

There are psychologists who believe that people need to get together, to be in some contact with each other, to relate.

People usually communicate with one another by talking, by simply looking at each other, by gestures, and by touching. The most common forms of communication involve talking. Probably the most intense involve touching.

People touch each other when they shake hands. People who play football touch each other in vigorous ways during the game. Hockey players touch one another, and so do boxers. Men and women involved in sexual activities touch each other.

■ It is easier to talk about the way people touch each other in a football game than it is to talk about the kinds of touching that can take place during intimate activities.

YES   (SEE PAGE 79.)

NO   (SEE PAGE 82.)

When men and women are involved in sexual activities, they usually pass through four phases of behavior. The first phase is sometimes called the phase of excitement.

For men, the phase of excitement typically occurs when the man is stimulated by a thought, an idea, a subjectively pleasing (for the individual male) sight, or when the penis itself is stimulated. During the excitement phase, the penis enlarges in size and this change is called an erection.

The woman's first response during the phase of excitement is the production of a body fluid that moistens and lubricates the inner surfaces of the vagina. The production of this fluid takes place because of indirect or direct stimulation of the genital region.

NOTE: Indirect stimulation for a woman is about the same sort of thing it is for a man. Indirect stimulation is brought about by a thought, an idea, a subjectively pleasing sight for the individual female. Direct stimulation involves touching.

■ During the excitement phase:

men require more stimulation than women. (TURN TO PAGE 80.)

women require more stimulation than men. (TURN TO PAGE 83.)

The second phase of behavior during sexual activities is called the plateau phase.

During the plateau phase, intercourse begins. The rate of breathing, normally between ten and sixteen breaths per minute, may go up to forty per minute. Normally the pulse rate is between sixty-five and seventy-five beats per minute, but during intercourse, the heart may beat one hundred and eighty times a minute or two beats every second. Blood pressure increases, and voluntary and involuntary muscles become tense.

During the plateau phase, the man and woman achieve a readiness for orgasm. Orgasm or climax is the third phase and it is the most intense of sexual experiences. The physiological aspects of sexual behavior are aimed at this goal, at orgasm.

During orgasm, pulse rate, breathing rate, and blood pressure reach a peak. Generalized perspiration may occur.

The fourth stage of sexual intercourse is often called the resolution phase. The orgasm leads to the release of muscular tension and the release of blood from the engorged blood vessels.

During the resolution phase both men and women relax, and pulse rate, breathing rate, and blood pressure return to normal.

After orgasm, men are somewhat unresponsive for varying lengths of time, usually several minutes. As the man grows older the length of time increases.

Women do not lose the ability to be sexually aroused during the resolution phase. Women can reach orgasm promptly when stimulation is renewed and can achieve several orgasms within a short period of time. In fact, some women find the second or third orgasm to be most satisfying.

■ Men and women experience orgasm at the same time.

TRUE   (SEE PAGE 81.)

FALSE   (SEE PAGE 84.)

Right, of course.

Once upon a time, legs were called limbs and birth was called "a blessed event." Young, unmarried women who were not considered virgins were labeled as "soiled doves." If a couple was seen kissing in the park, it was an automatic sign that they were either seriously engaged or recently married. The socially approved way of saying someone was pregnant was to describe her as "being in the family way." These were big city social ways and small town styles for dealing with the general subjects of intimacy and sex. On the frontier, though, conversations were usually more direct and earthy. Life was less civilized, less genteel, less inhibited on the frontier.

If someone had taken a survey a hundred years ago, the results would probably have shown that a small proportion of people knew a great deal about sex, a small proportion knew almost nothing, and most people were somewhere in between. If a survey were taken this year, the results would probably be about the same, if the survey dealt with what people knew about sex. If the survey dealt with what people did, and the frequency of sexual activities, the results would likely be different.

In spite of the influence of contemporary motion pictures, magazines, television shows, sex education lectures in public schools, etc., sex as a conversational topic can bring about more discomfort than is useful or necessary or appropriate. The discomfort seems to exist not only for single young people but also for married couples of all ages, for ministers and priests and rabbis who counsel, and for physicians as well.

TURN TO PAGE 77.

Your answer is wrong although there may be exceptions. Men enjoy sexual stimulation but generally need less in order to be ready for intercourse. Both men and women vary in sexual response and the quality and intensity of stimulation needed.

START OVER ON PAGE 77.

A false answer. You are wrong.

There is a mythology among numbers of people that the only adequate sort of sexual relationship that exists between a man and a woman is based on mutually and simultaneously achieved orgasms. While most people may wish to achieve orgasm at the same time, their wishes are not often fulfilled.

It is possible for a physical and sexual relationship to evolve to a strictly mechanical relationship in which both parties become sexual technicians rather than human beings involved in a close and potentially very intimate relationship.

Select the other answer on page 78.

Wrong.

The matter is so obvious, we would be surprised if anyone chose the "No" response.

If you did, go back to the "Yes" response on page 79 and read what is there.

You turned to the right page. Women seem to need more stimulation than men in the excitement phase.

This stimulation is frequently called foreplay. It involves touching the body in some manner to produce a pleasurable sensation. The most sensitive area is the genitalia. However, touching on any area of the body may produce a sexual response, depending on the desires of the woman and her feelings about her partner. For example, some women respond to stimulation of the breasts, and others do not find this enjoyable.

The woman needs to let the man know what is pleasurable to her. It is the man's responsibility to vary the foreplay so that intercourse can be a new and pleasant experience each time.

In addition to the amount and kind of stimulation, women usually need to feel love for the man in order to fully enjoy intercourse.

CONTINUE ON TO PAGE 78.

Correct. Men and women do not always experience an orgasm at the same time. People who feel their first sexual experience, say on the wedding night, will be a huge success may be disappointed. Achieving an orgasm for self and the partner takes practice and experience.

During intercourse, the man can move the penis back and forth inside the vagina. This movement causes friction, which stimulates the nerve endings in the head of the penis and similar nerve endings in the female genital organs. It is a complicated physiological process that may or may not lead to orgasm, particularly on a wedding night.

Achieving an orgasm also depends on such factors as emotional responses to the partner, how long since the last sexual experience, fear of pregnancy, the immediate environment, and how much the person has had to drink.

Because of ejaculation it is fairly obvious when men have reached orgasm. Women do not so overtly show response to orgasm. Women may enjoy sex even though they do not reach orgasm with their partner.

GO TO PAGE 85.

People can communicate with one another by talking, by looking at each other, by gestures, and by touching. It is possible, in sexual activities, to become involved in all of these ways of communicating.

Men and women achieve a high level of communication through sexual activities. They communicate with one another by talking, looking, gesturing, and touching. It is not, however, as simple as it may sound, for people are frequently anxious about sex and the anxiety may interfere with communication, with performance, and with enjoyment.

NOTE: Some of the time, people who are full of an endless repertory of jokes about sex are making an attempt to disguise anxiety over sexual matters. Some of the time, people who are unable to say anything at all about human sexual behavior may be anxious about that form of behavior.

It is not necessarily a sign of weakness or fear if an individual chooses to lead a life that does not include sexual behavior. There may be some individuals, however, who keep away from sexual activities because they have never been able to achieve satisfaction or pleasure of some sort no matter how diligently they tried. Some people may be so awed by sexual activities that they never even begin trying.

If people cannot obtain satisfaction from intercourse, they may feel they are impotent or frigid. Impotence refers to the male who cannot achieve an erection or who can maintain an erection only for a brief period of time. Frigidity generally means an inability to respond sexually to direct or indirect sexual stimulation. Frigidity is often used to describe a feminine form of impotence.

If there are no anatomical or physiological reasons for impotence or frigidity, and usually there are none, psychosexual feelings should be considered. Attitudes about sex, degree of attachment to or attraction for the sexual partner, fear of pregnancy, and past sexual experiences are important factors to consider if an individual feels impotent or frigid.

Sexual activity does not necessarily come to an end during the years of middle age or old age. Whether the older person participates in sexual activity depends more on his attitudes than on his physical state.

6

SELF-RELATIONSHIPS

She broke her leg less than two minutes after she'd gotten off the chair lift. The tip of her ski caught on something and she cartwheeled once before she slammed into a tree. The ski patrol took her down to the first aid cabin at the foot of the mountain. She rode back to the city in the back seat of a car, her leg in a temporary cast and her head in a morphine cloud.

In the emergency ward of the hospital, they cut away the temporary cast, x-rayed her leg, gave her another shot of morphine, and put on a new plaster cast. When they were finished with her, they wheeled her cart to an elevator and took her up to a room in the north wing of the hospital. Her sleep was a mixture of pain and drugs, but when she woke in the morning, she felt better. She wondered where her skiis and her ski boots were.

A doctor came to see her at ten o'clock that morning. He said she had a spiral fracture of the two bones in the lower part of her right leg. He told her she would have to stay in the hospital for a week and wear the heavy cast for three months. Then, if everything was all right, they would take the large cast off and put on a smaller one, which she would have to wear for another three months. He also told her that her skiis and ski boots had been stolen while she was in the first aid cabin.

She was a good patient during her stay in the hospital. She followed the nurse's orders. She ate the food and took the medications and smiled at friends who visited. She surprised everyone, however, when the doctor came by to sign the papers releasing her from the hospital. They greeted each other, he said good-by, and then she spit at him. He stepped back, wipping off his face as she apologized with a flurry of words. She felt ashamed and lonely.

All people are capable of anger.

Most people are apt to feel anger within themselves from time to time and will express at least some of what they feel. They may, however, use another word to describe what they are expressing.

The word *anger* is not a simple one to deal with. It can be used to describe a wide range of behavior. In addition, there are many words in the English language that are more acceptable to some people than "anger." They may be used in place of this word.

On a blank sheet of paper, list words that describe different degrees of anger. At the bottom of the scale, *feeling "put out"* might describe mild anger, while at the top *being in a rage* might describe great anger. Where would you locate words such as *irritated, bothered, "teed off,"* and *hateful?*

VERY HIGH LEVEL OF ANGER	12.	being in a rage
	11.	
	10.	
	9.	
	8.	
MODERATE LEVEL OF ANGER	7.	
	6.	
	5.	
	4.	
	3.	
	2.	
VERY LITTLE ANGER	1.	feeling "put out"

There are psychologists and psychiatrists who believe that one indicator of maturity is the ability to express legitimate anger. A few people, when they read that statement for the first time, may look around for something to be angry about. They do not have to look far.

Anger can result from frustration. *Frustration* is not a feeling. It is a condition. To be delayed or stopped in the pursuit of some goal is to be frustrated. Each of us experiences small frustrations every day. Sometimes, when we are in the greatest hurry, it seems the traffic lights magically change to red just before we get to them.

Every person has experienced frustration. For infants, frustration can be a delay in getting food when they are hungry. That delay, that frustration, can provoke a feeling of anger, which in infants is expressed by crying and kicking.

When infants evolve and grow to become children, they can tolerate delays a bit better, but if they are frustrated, the children may express anger by crying, hitting, screaming, or by breaking toys.

As children grow older, most of them develop more and more ability to tolerate frustration. At the same time, the children may be expected to handle their anger with more skill.

■ By the time an individual has achieved adulthood, he may be able to deal with a wide variety of daily frustrations. He may also be able to handle his anger in a more realistic manner.

AGREE   (SEE PAGE 93.)

DISAGREE (SEE PAGE 96.)

There are some adults who spend a lot of energy in an effort to hide the anger they feel. They may, when they are angry, smile. Others may cry when they are angry. Still others may become morose and depressed when the actual and real feeling they have is the feeling of anger. Most people, however, probably are more direct in expressing anger. Crying is almost always an expression of anger.

Think of the behavior of the bride's mother at the wedding. The bride's mother often cries sometime during the process of the marriage ceremony. It is almost a classic and predictable sort of behavior. The question, however, is "Why is she crying?" Perhaps she is angry because her daughter is leaving her. Perhaps she is angry because her daughter is young and has a chance at a long and happy marriage while she (the mother) fades from the scene into late middle age and old age. Maybe the mother is angry because the marriage ceremony reminds her that her dreams for a fully satisfying marriage were never met.

Think of someone who has just won an Oscar in the annual Academy Awards program. She may have won the award for her work in a great motion picture, and when she rises to accept the prize, she cries. In an indirect way, she may be saying, "Where were you when I needed you?"

It may be worth some time to think of the anger people express by crying at funerals, graduations, birthday parties, in happy movies, in sad movies, and during Fourth of July parades.

Newspaper reporters are usually aware of the capacity people have for expressing anger. Each murder, rape, and robbery is an expression of feelings of anger. Each newspaper story about murder, rape, and robbery is read with interest by thousands of people. The ordinary criminal may be a dull and uninteresting person until he commits a crime. Then he is an interesting person, not only to the police but to the rest of us as well.

Crime is interesting. Crime of one sort or another forms the basis for many popular television shows, best-selling books, and profit-making movies. A criminal, whether he is a fictional character in a story or a real person, is an individual who expresses anger in inappropriate ways.

Everyone is capable of anger. Everyone at some time or other has expressed anger in strong and direct ways. Infants, perhaps, do not regret the expression of anger when their food is delayed, but young children often regret the open expression of anger. Adults also often regret showing anger in open ways.

Anger and its expression can be troubling and anxiety provoking

89

for most people. However, the expression of anger may be less troubling than expressions of affection.

There are people who will, when they express anger, feel a sense of loneliness drift in on themselves. Some people may not express the anger; they may simply be aware of it within themselves, and that awareness may be followed by the development of a sense of isolation and loneliness. In such an instance, anger and loneliness are linked together.

Many people travel through life alone. To be alone is not the same as feeling lonely, but the two often go together.

To be alone is to be by oneself, and there may be many times when quiet privacy is preferred to companionship of any type.

To be lonely can sometimes mean being by oneself and hoping for and needing companionship but finding none. To be lonely can also mean being in a crowd, still hoping for and needing companionship, and still finding none.

If loneliness is based on hopes and needs that are not met, which of the following illustrates loneliness:

■ Bill lived alone. He usually went to the movies alone and he read books alone and worked in an office where he rarely spoke to anyone. When he did speak, he was reasonably friendly but the conversations were always short. He never got married and after he was 25, he never dated. He was always well mannered, polite, normally relaxed, and consistently a quiet man. He acted as though people were not important to him at all. (SEE PAGE 94.)

■ Jim lived alone. During the week he liked to read books and watch TV alone, but on weekends, he usually had a date. He drove a red Corvette and dated a different girl each weekend. He was always pleasant when he picked up his date, but near the end of the evening, he would usually become quiet and detached and sometimes morose. It was as if his date had disappointed him. On Mondays, he would go back to his job at the office. There, he was normally congenial, but if someone was not nice to him, he would seem to become temporarily sad or slightly angry. (SEE PAGE 98.)

In Chapter 1, the primal dialogue was mentioned. If a baby does not experience the primal dialogue, he may develop an anaclitic depression and die. An infantile anaclitic depression is an infant's response to an early-in-life and damaging form of loneliness. The opposite sort of infancy, in which the baby is raised with continual praise, admiration, and love will not result in an anaclitic depression, but it may lead to loneliness later in life.

If a baby is raised with nothing but praise (plus the necessary food and warmth), when all he gets is admiration and love, he may begin to believe that all of life is nothing but admiration and love. The baby may gradually develop a sense of identity that says he is omnipotent. He may not simply like himself but may love and adore himself as a baby, as a child, and, later, as an adolescent and as an adult.

A person who loves and adores himself and who expects others to continually do the same will not be welcomed as a companion by very many people. That person may not welcome anyone into his life unless the person he welcomes continually loves and adores him no matter what he may do. He will be lonely.

Reality testing is a common feature of daily living. For instance, if you want to test the reality of research findings in lung cancer, you may keep smoking and breathing smog and see what happens. If you sing in the shower and you sound wonderful, perhaps you could get a job singing opera at the Met. But, in order to test this reality, you would have to go through an audition and sing in front of experts, not in the shower. If you see a bowl filled with a white granular substance, you may believe it is salt or sugar. But to be absolutely certain, you would have to taste it. Reality testing would be tasting.

■ If you want to do some reality testing about loneliness, ask some friends if they have ever felt lonely.

If they are honest, chances are they will admit to feeling lonely some of the time. (SEE PAGE 95.)

If they are honest, chances are that a few will say they have felt lonely once or twice. (SEE PAGE 99.)

Loneliness can develop when the hopes and the needs for companionship are not met.

Most people hope for companionship, for the company and friendship of at least one and perhaps two or three other people in their lives. Most young adults are faced with the developmental task of achieving intimacy with a limited number of other people.

Companionship, intimacy, and, in general, relationships with other people can lead to the development of a clear awareness of oneself as a person, a maintenance of or an increase in the sense of personal identity. Loneliness will do just the opposite.

To describe being alone is simple. To describe or define loneliness is difficult. To describe or define the fear of loneliness may be impossible unless some attention is given to the way in which that fear may affect human behavior.

There are people who are almost always cooperative, consistently pleasant, and never controversial. They exert energy being friendly to everyone because they may believe that if they are not friendly they will be left alone, ignored, rejected, lonely.

Some people may be unfriendly almost all the time. They may be so antisocial that they end up with a long police record and spend years in jail. They may be rejected by society in general, but they certainly are not left alone or ignored.

■ Fear of loneliness may motivate different kinds of behavior.

AGREE   (SEE PAGE 97.)

DISAGREE (SEE PAGE 100.)

You are right.

By the time an individual has achieved adulthood, he should be able to deal with a large variety of frustrations. He should also be able to handle anger in a generally realistic way.

Children may be frustrated quite often because of the thousands of rules and regulations they must learn and follow. When a baby is born, he is an uncivilized savage. He must sooner or later learn table manners, cleanliness, a working vocabulary, how to sit still in a chair at school, how to get along cooperatively, and so on. Children are surrounded by rules that frustrate. This frustration will often cause anger to develop, but there are rules and regulations about anger, too.

The rules and regulations about handling anger are not as specific or as detailed as the rules and regulations concerned with table manners or toilet training. For many people, the rule is "Don't" with regard to anger. Many parents are able to show their children how to behave during a meal, but not as many parents seem skilled in showing their children how to deal with anger. Many times, parents are apt to convey the idea that anger is wrong. Children can grow into adults who feel the same way.

GO NOW TO PAGE 89.

Bill's style of living does not illustrate loneliness. He is alone much of the time, but he may be so consistently self-sufficient or so thoroughly sealed off from other people that he does not feel loneliness at all.

There may not be many people who live so comfortably and so alone.

Read about loneliness on page 98.

Yes, the chances are that all people will admit to feeling lonely some of the time, especially if they are honest about their feelings.

Loneliness is a feeling people have. Some people are aware of having the feeling more often than others. Most people (perhaps including some friends) may not admit to loneliness because such an admission is an unpopular sort of thing.

It is possible for mature people to honestly express anger and affection, but how does a person express loneliness? To talk about loneliness is not easy, for that can mean admitting to rejection by another person. Talking about loneliness may also bring to mind the television commercials about bad breath or body odor or some other superficial human characteristic. To be lonely may mean not only being unpopular but also being ignored, overlooked, forgotten, lost, abandoned.

Loneliness develops out of a hope and a need for companionship. Loneliness develops when the hopes and needs are not met. Those words may partially define the development of loneliness, but they do not define loneliness itself.

TURN TO PAGE 92.

Wrong.

Adults typically should be able to handle frustration and anger in ways that are more realistic than the manner in which these factors in living are handled by children.

START OVER ON PAGE 88.

To agree this time is correct.

Yes, fear of loneliness may motivate different kinds of behavior.

Further on in this book (Chapter 11), you will find a discussion of anxiety. Anxiety and the avoidance of anxiety can also motivate different kinds of human behavior. It may be that anxiety and fear of loneliness are often the same feeling.

The next chapter starts on page 101.

Jim's style of living illustrates loneliness. You are right in choosing this alternative.

From the brief paragraph about Jim, you may have become aware that he feels disappointed in people when they are not "nice" to him. He may have been consistently disappointed with his dates because they were never nice enough to him. Maybe he would have been pleased with a date who continually praised him, praised his car, and admired him in an unquestioning way. But a date who acted that way would not have been realistic in her actions. For Jim to expect such actions would be unrealistic.

Go on to page 91, where you can read about the sort of background Jim might have had and why he might have felt lonely.

No.

If only a few will admit they have felt lonely once or twice, either they have not been honest about their feelings or you are talking with people who know very little about themselves.

GO BACK TO PAGE 91.

This time to disagree is wrong.

Go back to page 92. Try the other alternative. In the meantime, however, keep in mind that some loneliness seems to be a part of living. Loneliness, to some degree, may be as much a part of being human as feeling anger is, or affection, or having bones and skin.

To be afraid of loneliness may be understandable. It may be logical, especially if the reasons behind the fear are known. And, although fear of loneliness is understandable and its development a logical part of a person's life history, fear of loneliness may be as irrational as fear of the dark or fear of black cats.

Some people join organizations in order to be with other people, at least for some of the time of their lives. Some people do not join organizations, not so much because they are not joiners, but because they have difficulty in leaving the organization. Parting for them, may be painful.

If you were forced to place yourself among the joiners or the nonjoiners, in which group would you find yourself?

Now go back to page 92.

7

THE FAMILY: TASK AND PROCESS

He was a big man, older than the others. He was big with a layer of fat that showed in his thick wrists and in his face and in his belly that stuck out, pulling at the buttons on his shirt and stretching his belt. He was big and fat and powerful and the others knew his strength.

He was a foreman in the mill and he'd won every fight he'd had there, won every dispute that challenged his power over men and they knew it. His hands were tremendous, gnarled, with a look about them as though they'd been rough-chiseled out of granite or formed from concrete. When he curled his thick fingers and balled them into a fist, his fist reminded the others of the head of a sledgehammer.

With the side of his fist, he steadily pounded out a slow, marching rhythm on the lowered steel tailgate of the large truck and with his other hand he wiped the rain from his eyes and pressed the water out of the thick hair on the back of his thick neck. With his reddened eyes, he watched the others move to the steady, heavy beat of his fist; and when he sensed they were slowing down, he would match the sound of the pounding with his hoarse, rumbling voice and he would say,

Go . . . Go . . . Go . . . Go . . . Go . . . Go . . .

The others moved numbly to his measured cadence, dark figures working like exhausted robots as the rain came down on them. Two men stood in the back of the truck, moving the sandbags toward the tailgate. The men on the ground came one at a time to the back of the truck, where they would pull a sandbag onto a shoulder and carry it through the rain to the levee, which held back the surging waters of the flooded river. They had been working for four days now, living in a cold, unending rain, loading the truck at the sandpit, riding in the back to the edge of the swirling, muddy river, where they unloaded the truck, piling the sandbags to make a thick, two-mile wall meant to save the town from a wild flood that would tear everything away from them.

Two thousand men worked in the cold, steady rain. A hundred crews labored, each with a head man whose job it was to keep people moving, working, doing the things that had to be done to save the town with its homes and churches and school. Two thousand men worked for six days at the sandpit, on trucks and along the river. In the end, they preserved the town. Two thousand men worked themselves to exhaustion; but when they were rested and recovered and when their world dried out, they had the biggest party anyone of them could remember. And, at the feast, no one was loved more than the big man with sledgehammer hands.

The world is full of groups of people. Some groups are large; they occupy a certain area of land and are called nations. Some groups are small. They occupy a house or a grass hut or a cave and are called families.

A group of people will stay together as long as they have something in common, whether it is the work they do, the games they play, or the land they live on.

A group of people with interests and objectives in common form an organization. Families are organizations. So are Girl Scout troops, Marine brigades, emergency flood control crews, and corporations. Every organization is composed of people who have ideas, thoughts, opinions, beliefs, feelings, and attitudes.

Almost all organizations, including families, will have and must have (if they are to endure) a headship position. The headship position is a position with some power, influence, and control over those who occupy the lower layers in the organization. The headship position has responsibility and the "right" to give orders. Parents have power and influence over their children. Parents are responsible for their own children, to whom they give orders.

Headships are granted to parents by society, and that includes the school systems, the landlord, the cruising policeman, and the little league football coach.

Headship positions are not the same as leadership positions. Headship positions are granted by society. In a family setting, leadership positions are granted to parents by the children.

■ The position of headship is essentially given to those who are willing to accept certain responsibilities and rights. Leadership positions, in one way or another, are earned.

AGREE   (SEE PAGE 109.)

DISAGREE (SEE PAGE 112.)

Any organization (including the family) must take care of the essential duties. In a family the essential duties or *necessary tasks* involve getting the food and the clothing, when those are needed, and finding and keeping a place to live (which means a place where the food is prepared and eaten, a place where people may sleep, a place where they may take care of the more personal matters as in a bathroom).

Essential duties, the necessary tasks of organizational life, can be listed. Some of them are mentioned in the paragraph above. On a blank page, write those tasks down and add some that have not been mentioned. Keep in mind that you are making a list of the tasks, the basic activities, that are supposed to provide for the physical, physiological survival of the members of a small organization we can call a family. Keep in mind, also, that essential tasks do not involve buying tickets for a show or getting someone to install wall-to-wall carpets. These may be tasks, but they are not necessary for the physical and physiological survival of the members of a small organization.

It may be possible to list fifty or a hundred tasks that are essential to the survival of a small family organization. It may, in addition, be possible to list several thousand different, common, and nonessential tasks. Each task, whether it is essential or nonessential, will be linked with what has been called *process*. Each task will be linked to feelings.

The linkage of task and process is often overlooked in small organizations and in large conglomerate organizations. Under some circumstances, to know the linkage or connection can be useful in understanding the organization and in the development of one's own sense of personal identity.

Task and process are linked together. The task is often easier to identify than the process. Sometimes the task is so critical that process is all but ignored. For instance, the head man on the flood control work group put considerable pressure on his men to accomplish the task to which they were assigned (moving sandbags from the pit to the levee). Process was temporarily unimportant and was ignored or pushed aside because of the emergency conditions.

In families, there may be times when process is ignored, pushed aside, made temporarily unimportant because of special conditions that are sometimes emergencies. If a house is burning down around them, who in the family will stop to ponder the feelings they have about the task of escaping? Who would pause to reflect on the feelings they have about themselves and other people as they run from the flames and smoke?

■ Process is ignored or pushed aside only under conditions of extreme and severe emergency.

AGREE (SEE PAGE 110.)

DISAGREE (SEE PAGE 113.)

Process and task are linked together. Sometimes the process is so momentarily critical or overriding that task is all but ignored. For instance, if a girl of about age 5 is asked by her mother to carry out the garbage (a task), her playtime may be interrupted by the chore. If that impending interruption is the most recent of a long series of delays in experiencing pleasure (a delay can be a frustration) for that little girl, she may rapidly fall to the floor, kick her feet, scream, and cry in a display of temper (a symptom of process). In this instance, process overrides the task. Process and not the task becomes the problem. Task is ignored, at least temporarily.

■ Task may be ignored or at least temporarily pushed aside if a person's feeling about the task, about himself, and about the other people involved becomes strong.

YES   (SEE PAGE 111.)

NO   (SEE PAGE 116.)

Conflict between the bottom layer and the top layer is not necessarily inevitable, but it can develop if there are large enough changes in the environment in which people live.

To return to an idea expressed earlier in this book: The adolescents and young adults of today were born into and have experienced a world vastly different from the world their parents once knew. The difference is great enough to foster the development of different views and values and ideals. The differences lead to a gap between generations.

The gap between the bottom and the top layers in a contemporary family may be greater and have more effect on behavior than the gap between bottom and top layers in most other two-layered organizations.

If the environment changes, as it has in the twentieth century, the people who live in that environment will find themselves involved in changed activities.

A change in activities means a change in what people do. The children and adolescents of today are often engaged in activities that are vastly different from the activities their parents experienced when the parents were much younger.

The differences between generations seem, in the main, to involve differences in what people do, what their activities are. (The differences in activities may lead to differences in feelings about self, others, and tasks.) The basis of the gap between generations begins with a change in environment, which leads to changes in what people do, and those changes may or may not lead to changes in the way people feel.

■ The generation gap may show up in process, but it is apparently based on and developed out of changes in task.

AGREE   (SEE PAGE 114.)

DISAGREE   (SEE PAGE 117.)

The gap between the bottom and the top layers in a family may affect and influence process, but that gap may originate because of differences in task.

It may be that the bottom and top layers in a family agree on tasks that are essential to the survival of that small organization. However, they may not agree on the common but nonessential tasks. The matter becomes complicated if the same task is viewed as essential by some families and nonessential by other families. There is, for example, the matter of education.

Some parents view education of any sort as unimportant, too much trouble, or a waste of time. Their children may introject such attitudes and have difficulties in getting through grade school and high school. Other parents may believe strongly in the value of an education, and, if the children introject, the children may complete school. (Some children will, of course, be negativistic or self-defeating about the whole matter.)

■ To complete high school or college is to complete a long series of tasks. While parents may agree with their children about the value of an education, there may be disagreement about the tasks involved. Schools may require the younger generation to accomplish tasks that are different from the tasks the parents accomplished while they were in school. This difference may affect and influence process within the family organization.

AGREE   (SEE PAGE 115.)

DISAGREE (SEE PAGE 118.)

You are right.

Leadership is earned, not given. Parents, if they wish to be leaders, must earn that position in one manner or another. In a sense, the same arrangement exists in a corporation. The supervisor is given a position of headship when he is promoted to the job of supervisor. He is not in a position of leadership until his employees accept him as their leader.

Headship is concerned with organizational duties. Organizational duties in a family involve such things as getting enough food, finding some place to live, washing dishes, and so on. Organizational duties are the more formal matters of family life and they can be called the tasks.

Leadership involves relationships between people, and it is concerned with the personal and emotional factors of living. Personal and emotional factors are sometimes called process.

Any organization (including the family) must handle the necessary tasks and somehow deal with the process.

Tasks are what people do. Process refers to how people feel about what they do and how they feel about themselves and each other.

Several generations ago, parents, presidents, and supervisors may have believed that tasks were far more important than process. Now, however, a great deal of attention is given to the way people feel about what they do and how they feel about each other. Corporations and families seem increasingly aware that process is critical in the life of the organization.

TURN TO PAGE 104.

Do you agree? You are in error if you do.

Process is ignored, pushed aside, covered over, denied, suppressed, and somehow treated as unimportant in many circumstances and situations.

NOTE: Task is often easier to define than process. Many times, task is simpler to deal with than process, especially for the people involved in the task and engaged in the process.

Read page 105 once more, then select the other answer.

Yes, of course.

There may be times when task is pushed aside, ignored, or overlooked if process becomes strong.

You may recall some of the comments about self-defeating behavior made earlier (Chapter 2). Go back to page 23; then move on to page 36 for three examples of self-defeating behavior. Each example depicts process overriding task.

NOW PROCEED ON PAGE 107.

You are wrong.

Leadership is earned, not given.

No one can be a leader of a group unless the group accepts that individual as the leader.

Read more about this on page 109.

You are correct if you disagree.

Process is ignored or pushed aside in many circumstances and situations. This ignoring and pushing aside may be more obvious in families than in most other organizations.

Families are small organizations that have at least two layers. The top layer (parents) is separated from the bottom layer (children) by a gap that sometimes resembles a battlefield. Sometimes the gap may look like a peaceful meeting ground. Many times, however, the gap between the top and bottom layers (between generations) is ignored, covered over, denied, or treated as unimportant.

In most organizations, perhaps especially in the family, task is easier to define than process. Task is often simpler to deal with than process. How people feel about each other and about themselves and how they feel about what they do is usually more complex and certainly more personal than what they do. Think about the sort of bare and sterile conversation two people can have when they discuss only a specific task. When process enters the conversation, the discussion may become livelier.

CONTINUE ON PAGE 106.

You are correct.

Changes in tasks seem to be at the core of the causes for a generation gap.

If you have enjoyed total agreement on all things with your parents, you may not have experienced the gap between your generation and theirs. Maybe you have a friend who will describe to you some areas of disagreement he may have had with his parents. You might begin by asking him about what his parents did, how they lived, what their activities were while they were growing up. Then you might ask him to contrast the parental activities during their childhood with his own activities during his early years. If you can get that far, you have what may be the beginnings of a conversation about the generation gap.

TURN TO PAGE 108.

Correct. You are right to agree.

The differences in the tasks called for by schools can affect and influence process within the family organization.

Within a family, there are many differences between the two generations. Children and parents differ, of course, in age and experience. The older generation is older, and they may often remind the younger generation of the fact. The older generation has more experience in living (or at least in being alive) than the younger generation, and that will be brought up from time to time. Yet, the older generation may often wish to be young again. They may also wish they could have experienced what young people experience in accomplishing tasks today. This may be more obvious in connection with education than in a number of other areas.

When people graduate now from high school, they have experienced a long series of small tasks that are usually more difficult, more sophisticated, and more demanding than the experiences their parents had in high school. The high school graduate of today has a substantially better education than the high school graduate of 20 or 30 years ago. Many parents may feel uneasy in quiet or noisy ways about this. They may sometimes believe that the advances their children make put them (the parents) in a bad light. They may feel uncomfortable if their children accomplish more than they did at the same period in their lives. Some children may, in addition, avoid or belittle their own accomplishments in order to keep peace with their parents. They may do this if they have overpracticed the art of losing.

You are now ready for the next chapter. Turn to page 119.

If you think the answer is "No," you are wrong.

Task may be ignored or at least temporarily pushed aside if process becomes overriding. Task may be all but forgotten in the heat or cold of emotion.

START OVER ON PAGE 106.

You are wrong this time.

If you do not feel certain about the conflict between the bottom and top layers in a family organization, you may need to reread portions of this chapter. If you are unsure about the idea of the generation gap, perhaps you can review some of the ideas in Chapter 2 on adolescence.

Then go to page 107 and try again.

You are wrong.

Perhaps you need to reread page 108 before going on to the correct response. Keep in mind the distinction between task and process.

8
THE SCHOOL

He hated school. He hated the doorways and the floors and the pictures on the walls. He hated the school building and the teachers, but most of all he hated the work they assigned to him. There was too much of it, he thought. There was too much to learn, and he sometimes wondered if he would get through it all.

He was filled with a bad feeling about homework. It took up most of his time in the evening. If he fell behind, his father made him stay at home all weekend, memorizing, reading, talking with his mathematics tutor, and working out problems in design. He would rather go swimming or walk around town with his friends.

For the past year, all the design problems had to do with the shape and style of triangles. Next year, he knew, he would advance to structural design, and they would teach him how to combine triangles so they fit together in mathematically precise ways.

He wished for summer. When summer came, he would go south with his family to their summer home in the cool mountains. They would travel on the river in a large boat, and he could stand on the platform in the stern, looking down at the slaves who rowed the boat. He knew the boat passed by the place where he would spend most of his life after he'd finished school. He knew he'd look up then and gaze past the flat bank of the river to the land that lay beyond. He would picture in his mind the size and shape of the pyramid he was to design. Even then, he would wonder why the Pharaoh had chosen him to be Master Architect.

No one knows, with any degree of sureness, when schools were invented. Perhaps they slowly developed within the family of the caveman. Dressed in animal skins and covered with insect bites and thorn scratches, the cave-dwelling father may have grunted instructions to his cave-dwelling son in the art of stealing honey from the bees or showed the boy where to find wild duck eggs or how to catch fish with his bare hands.

The caveman father and his son were in a two-layered organization, and each was involved in teaching and learning the accomplishment of tasks essential to the survival of the organization. Schools may not be much different from that now.

Each classroom has people in it who are members of a two-layered organization. The students occupy the bottom layer. The teacher is the top layer.

In important ways, parents influence the behavior of their children, and the influence will show up in the child's behavior at school.

Success or failure at school can be based on the student's general level of intelligence, a factor that seems partly a matter of heredity and partly a matter of environmental experiences. Success or failure at school can also be based on the attitudes the parents have about school, schooling, and education in general.

Some parents view schools as unimportant. Other parents may strongly believe in education and put such a high value on school and schooling that almost everything else is secondary.

Children can be expected to take on the beliefs and attitudes of their parents. This may not always be the case; but if parents place a high value on school, the children usually will, too. If parents place a low value on school, the children will usually do the same.

Introjection operates in ways that have already been mentioned (Chapter 1). Typically, children will take on the beliefs and attitudes of their parents, and this includes beliefs and attitudes parents have about school. If, however, the parents merely talk about the importance of school and then never visit the school or ask about it or listen to their children when they talk about school, the children may get the idea that the parents do not mean it when they say school is important. Also, there may be some children who respond negativistically to their parents and perhaps to many other people. If the parents say school is important, negativistic children may find enjoyment of a sort in downgrading the importance of school.

Success or failure at school can be based not only on family attitudes about the value of school but also on the development, among other things, of language behavior in the home.

120

The development of language behavior in the home is related to the level of success the family organization has in achieving essential tasks.

Some essential tasks are the same from one family to the next. They involve getting enough food, finding a place to live, etc.

If the top layer in the family organization has had less than average success in the accomplishment of essential tasks, the family may not have enough space in which to live in some comfort. They may live crowded together simply because they cannot afford to live in more spacious surroundings.

■ When the family organizations live crowded together in one or two rooms, people eat, sleep, talk, argue, laugh, and watch television, and all of this activity generates sound. An infant who lives and sleeps in such a crowded home may hear so much sound that sounds begin rapidly to lose their meaning. When he vocalizes, he may not be heard and he may not be responded to. When his mother talks to him, the sound of her voice may be lost amidst all the other sounds in the room. As a result, his understanding of spoken words and their meanings may not develop adequately. He may be handicapped in the development of his language behavior because of his parents' inability to accomplish essential tasks well enough to ensure a certain amount of privacy and quiet some of the time.

YES (SEE PAGE 125.)

NO (SEE PAGE 128.)

To "fit in" at school can mean the student successfully develops satisfactory working relationships with teachers and with other students. To "fit in" can also mean to conform, to compromise, to surrender a part of one's independence to the school system. Both meanings apply.

Students who do well in school ordinarily form adequate (or at least passable) relationships with others at school and they conform to the system. This is most obviously the case in kindergarten and first grade.

In the fall of every year, about 3 million children start school for the first time. For almost all of them, it is the first time they have had to contend with an environment in which the rules and the expectations are written down. By the time a student reaches junior high school, he usually has the system figured out and he knows, generally, what his freedoms are and what they are not. And it is at this time that he begins to seriously question the relevance of the process we call education. He may begin to openly question why he must learn certain things, and he may wonder why he cannot either safely ignore school or study only those subjects or areas he himself wants to learn about. He may, in effect, begin to rebel against the system to which he has so easily conformed for 6, 7, or 8 years.

■ In general, conformity has its drawbacks, but it is a necessary aspect of school.

If that is your opinion, see page 126.

■ In general, conformity to a school system is harmful.

If that is your opinion, see page 129.

When the individual expands his life and enters the school environment, he enters the first (for him) environment in which the rules and expectations are written down. There is, in most school systems, a charter or a statement of the purpose and, often, a set of bylaws for the school board. There usually is a policy paper to be followed by the administrators, the staff experts, and the teachers. There are, more specifically, contracts drawn up by the system to which principals and teachers put their signatures. In addition, there are course outlines and curriculum guides, schedules and classroom teaching strategies, grading standards, required tasks and courses, student conduct codes, policies on absence and tardiness, and student government rules.

In addition to formally recognized rules and expectations, there are the less formal rules and regulations enforced by the individual teacher in the classroom. The less formal or informal rules may have to do with specific conduct in the room, what the teacher will allow or not allow when the students talk to her, and the way in which students deal with each other in the classroom.

Almost every teacher will have a reasonably good awareness of the formal school rules. And almost every teacher will follow the rules and expect students to do the same. In addition, the teacher will have her own rules, which students are expected to learn and to follow. The rules the teacher has are personal, usually subjective, sometimes based on experience; but in any case their personal nature makes them important. The teacher may have had very little to say about the rules the school system has. But she has had quite a bit to say about the rules she has developed, and she may enforce these personal rules more strictly because they are hers. Because they are her own rules, the teacher will expect the student to put a high value on them; but if the student does not (that is, if he does not conform), the teacher may react negatively.

There are differences between the rules of behavior at home and in the neighborhood and the rules of behavior at school. One difference, which has already been touched on, is that many of the rules at school are written down while the rules of behavior at home and in the neighborhood usually are not. Another difference is that the rules at school change from year to year. The ones at home and in the neighborhood often do not.

There is, in most families, a kind of stability, a permanence or rigidity, in the relations people have with each other. Parents may often develop a set pattern for relating with a child, and that pattern may not change much from year to year. How the parents and the child interact when the child is 6 may be how they interact when the child is 16. The limits placed on the child (the familial rules and regulations) may not change much over the years. At school they do.

The class schedules in the early years of school are tight, and it is usual for them to be closely adhered to, not only by the teacher but also by the small students. There are few choices open to the first grader. He must work on his reading and his writing. He usually must paint or cut and paste at a certain time. He must have recess when the schedule permits it. He must not throw snowballs at other children. By contrast, the typical high school senior can choose at least one and sometimes two or three subjects to take that are not required subjects. He can often, if he chooses, talk openly with teachers about a variety of topics, although he still cannot throw snowballs on school property without getting into trouble.

■ Home and family environments transmit information to the individual. The school environment also transmits information to the individual. Which environment is most effective; which transmits the most information?

HOME   (SEE PAGE 127.)

SCHOOL   (SEE PAGE 130.)

Yes, you are right.

One of the factors that seem to help in learning is the distinctiveness of the material to be learned.

If an infant lives in a poor setting, surrounded by all kinds of noise, the sounds that make up words are lost, mixed in with all the other sounds in the room. In contrast, if a family organization has managed to accomplish the essential tasks well enough, the people in the family may have plenty of space in which to eat, sleep, talk, and so on. They are not apt to be crowded into one or two rooms. The infant may have his own room, and the sounds of words may be clear and distinct to him.

If the infant can experience times of quiet and if that silence is broken by his mother's voice, the impact of the sound will be far greater than if it is just another voice speaking in a room filled with noisy people. The words his mother says will, because of that impact, take on greater meaning. The infant, in effect, will not be dulled to sound or distracted by other sounds and he will learn more rapidly and with more precision what his mother says to him. He will, in effect, get a head start on learning the language because he has a quiet place in which to live. That he does have a quiet and uncrowded living space may be based on the success his parents have had in achieving tasks.

Go to page 122 for the next series.

Right.

Conformity is a necessary aspect of school. (It is also a necessary aspect of living in a family.) No one can learn to read and write without some attention to schedules and demands of teachers and principals. It is not possible, in a reasonably democratic society, to educate large masses of citizens unless those citizens give up some of their time and certain sectors of their freedom in order to become educated. This may not be as wholly true at the collegiate level as it is during the primary and secondary school levels.

PROCEED TO PAGE 123.

You are wrong.

The home environment does not transmit more information to the individual. The school does. This may not have been the case for the cave-dwelling father, who taught his son the tasks essential to the survival of the family organization, but it is the case now.

Perhaps as recently as several generations ago, the people in the home setting may have transmitted more information to the child than the school did. Now, however, schools transmit more.

RETURN TO PAGE 124.

No. You are wrong.

Go back and try again on page 121.

Wrong.

Conformity, in general, is not harmful to students in a school system. In specific instances, however, conformity may work to the disadvantage of some students.

START OVER ON PAGE 122.

Right.

The school environment transmits far more information to the individual than the home environment does.

Several generations ago, the father taught his son all that the son needed to know to make a living. The mother taught her daughter all she needed to know in order to get married and keep house and raise children. It is not the same now. What the father knows is not often useful to the son. How the father lives and the kind of man he is may be useful, but not what he knows. The information the father has now is generally either too specialized and technical to transmit to the son or is the sort that will be obsolete by the time the son is old enough to use it on any job. So the information and knowledge that are transmitted to the younger generation are transmitted, typically, by the school system.

9

FORMAL
ORGANIZATION
AND
LEADERSHIP

She was a secretary. She worked for the president of the firm, and he demanded, and got, a lot of work from her. She was paid more than a foreman in the factory and twice as much as any manager in any one of the sixty-seven branch offices scattered around the country.

She had a large teakwood desk and a pale blue push-button telephone. Her electric typewriter matched the telephone. Her desk and chair rested on a gold colored carpet that reminded her, some of the time, of the wheat fields on the farm where she'd grown up.

Whenever she remembered the fields of wheat, she recalled her father. He was a big, boisterous man who liked to laugh and sing and who always had a look of great pleasure on his face whenever he hugged her mother, which seemed to be most of the time. She wished the president could be like that once in a while. He was always busy, moving quickly from one project to the next, smiling because he was polite, not because he felt happy.

She wished he would hug her, just once, but she knew he never would. He was too careful with himself and too well mannered when he talked with her, self-conscious in a way, but aware of the power he had as president of the firm. She wondered why he didn't have the power to enjoy himself as her father had.

Families are organizations. Schools are organizations. Most families are informal organizations; but schools, in contrast, are formal. They have charters, policy statements, procedures, forms, and reports of various types. In addition, schools employ people who have been trained to do the work they do.

Schools are formal organizations. So are infantry regiments, electronics corporations, and hospitals. Formal organizations place a heavy emphasis on "getting the job done."

All formal organizations are composed of people. People have a great assortment of ideas, thoughts, opinions, beliefs, feelings, and attitudes. None of these are easily shared by members of organizations. Formal organizations may not want such things shared or brought into the open. To do so might interfere with getting the job done.

Formal organizations emphasize not only task but also behavior that is logical and rational.

Members of formal organizations, whether the organization is a bank, a trucking company, or a school system, are not usually allowed to express emotions (which are often illogical) in an open and free manner. The members are expected to do their jobs in a rational manner, in a predictable way, typically going through a series of logical steps that are often outlined in a procedures manual.

Members of formal organizations are often expected to accomplish tasks regardless of what the emotional process may be.

If task is paramount and process is viewed with raised eyebrows, members of formal organizations are apt to hide their feelings, to disguise or deny the positive and negative feelings they will inevitably have.

The infantry regiment, the trucking company, and other formal organizations have systems of rewards and punishments. People will be promoted, fired, transferred, or simply ignored, according to the way in which they behave. Rewards are typically given to people who attend carefully to the job that must be done and who perform in an apparently logical and rational manner. Punishment, on the other hand, is meted out to those who act illogically (even if they do so for only a very brief period of time) or who openly express antiorganization sentiments too often.

Formal organizations usually emphasize task, and they normally expect and typically reward behavior that is aimed primarily at the central goal of getting the job done.

Formal organizations often seem to have little use for process. They often place a low value on feelings and emotions that do not directly connect with the main goal of getting the job done. It is as

132

though the top layers in formal organizations believe that process may interfere with the work that, of necessity, must be done.

Under these circumstances, people who are members of formal organizations may swiftly learn to deny, disguise, hide, or suppress much of what can be called process.

When people attend mainly to task and when process is not dealt with, many facets of interpersonal relationships will remain undeveloped.

■ If many facets of interpersonal relationships remain undeveloped, people will typically:

get along in one way or another, but they may not really like each other. (SEE PAGE 137.)

not really solve interpersonal problems in a mature or generally lasting way. (SEE PAGE 140.)

Formal organizations grant headship positions to some of their members. Headship positions are called foreman or supervisor or manager.

Some of the people who are given headship positions attend only to task while overlooking or ignoring or suppressing process. Others, however, may deal with both task and process.

If a person in a headship position can accomplish task and, at the same time, effectively deal with process, he may evolve to a leadership position.

A person who occupies a leadership position must deal with process and with the feelings people have about the task, about themselves, and about each other. He must deal with process in an open manner. To do so successfully may depend on the development of his own sense of personal identity.

Most formal organizations are faced with the problem of getting people to do their work.

People who are in headship positions may be able to get people to work, but their techniques and strategies are probably limited.

■ People in leadership positions may have:

about the same sort of techniques and strategies as people in headship positions have. (TURN TO PAGE 138.)

a greater variety of techniques and strategies for getting people to do their work. (TURN TO PAGE 141.)

Control by direct order is frequently used in organizing people, not only by those in headship positions but also by those who have managed to achieve a position of leadership.

Meaningful control by direct order is usually backed up by some form of authority. The authority, in this case, is the authority or the power or the "right" to punish. Ordinarily, a direct order cannot be given safely unless it is backed up, either by the power inherent in a formal organization or by the sort of power one man may have over another by way of muscle, intelligence, money, seniority, or position.

Control by direct order is simple, direct, and crude. It is, in many situations, the sort of control necessary when speed of response to that control is important.

A person who occupies a headship position may more often resort to control by direct order than may a person who occupies a leadership position. If speed of response is important, however, control by way of direct order will be the best form to use, no matter who is in the top layer. Also, control by direct order will be the most workable sort if those who are controlled rank well below the person who controls.

Control by competition is not nearly as crude or as specifically based as control by direct order.

Control of behavior by setting up a competition is an old technique. The sales manager can design a sales contest and salesmen may compete for the prize. Their behavior is controlled by the competition.

Corporations compete with each other for the market, and football teams compete for the championship. Drag racers compete, as do swimming teams, armies, and nations.

Do you compete? Perhaps. Is some aspect of your life affected by competition somewhere? Of course.

On a blank page, write out one aspect of your life that has been influenced by some form of competition.

Put down the way in which some part of your life has been influenced by competition between two companies, two schools, or two nations.

Think about a competition in which you had a part, no matter how remote. What did you feel when you won in the competition? If you lost, what did you feel?

Control by consultation is sophisticated.

Consultation refers to communications between the people involved in the controlling and those who are controlled.

135

The leader of a group may present a problem to his group for discussion. The group may discuss ways of solving the problem. At some time or other, the leader pulls in the loose ends of the discussion, summarizes what has been said, and, often with the group's help, outlines the best solution that has been brought up in the meeting.

In a sense, control by consultation is a very loose and almost democratic form of control. It works slowly and may be useful when there is time for a discussion.

Control by consultation operates at a slower pace than control by direct order.

Control by direct order may be the most useful technique if those who are controlled have modest skills or if they rank well below the level of the person who controls.

Control by consultation generally works if the members of the discussion can all contribute something to the solution of a given problem. This means that control by consultation will not work very well with highly unskilled people who are faced with a complicated problem that only skilled people could solve.

When King Arthur formed the Round Table and invited the best of knights to sit with him to work out the problems of the realm, he developed control through consultation. Legend has it that the Round Table meetings eventually failed because of rivalries and jealousies between knights. Process overrode task.

King Arthur did not originate consultation, Christ did not, nor did Moses. Where it began, and when, remains unknown, but it has developed and evolved through the centuries and the generations to become a useful technique, a generally practical strategy in the solution of many different kinds of organizational problems.

Control by consultation is sophisticated, and it seems most useful in settings in which all the people involved have skills and abilities that can be brought to bear on the problems to be solved.

■ Control by consultation is somewhat risky. While the consultative approach is aimed mainly at task, process may override task.

If you agree, see page 139.

■ Control by consultation is necessary and should be the preferred method of dealing with organization problems in all settings.

If you agree, see page 142.

Well, you may be correct, but the other choice is a better one.

If interpersonal relationships remain undeveloped, people may somehow manage to get along in one way or another. They will get along in a superficial manner, however, and relationships between them are apt to cause dissatisfaction or at least bring about a strong sense that something is missing. The missing factor may be depth of relationships or the development of meaningful relationships.

Read the correct response on page 140.

You are wrong.

Headship and leadership are different in some aspects. One of these differences involves the way in which headship people and leadership people motivate those who work for them.

Leadership people have, typically, a wider choice of ways that they may use in getting people to do the work that needs to be done.

Return to page 134 and start over.

Yes.

You are right to think that control by consultation can be risky. The risk involves taking the chance that process will override task. Because of that risk, control by consultation may be best used by supervisors and managers who operate along a leadership dimension rather than along a headship dimension.

The next chapter begins on page 143.

You are right.

If interpersonal relationships remain undeveloped, people will typically not solve interpersonal problems in mature or lasting ways.

In formal organizations, interpersonal relationships will usually be based on task and on process. People will be put together in groups in order to accomplish task. If all they do is deal with task, they may get the job done, but they may not do even that if process is ignored or suppressed. Keep in mind that process can override task in more ways than in the example of the little girl who throws a tantrum and who, because of that, does not carry out the garbage (Chapter 7).

If process is not dealt with, the feelings may come into the open in a variety of subtle and unsubtle ways.

If process is not dealt with, the feelings will not simply go away.

GO TO PAGE 134.

You are right.

Leadership people may have a greater variety of techniques and strategies for getting people to do their work.

It may be that all the techniques, all the organizational and personal strategies, that are designed to get people to do what must be done can be reduced to three forms of control:

1. Control by direct order
2. Control by competition
3. Control by consultation

Go to page 135 and begin reading about these forms of control. Your life may often be affected by one or the other of these three.

No.

You are incorrect if you believe control by consultation is necessary and preferred.

The type of control used depends on the sort of people involved, their level of skill, the supervisory or managerial talent level, and the kinds of problems that need to be solved. Time is also important. Control by consultation is a slow process compared with control by direct order.

START OVER ON PAGE 136.

10

THE BIG SCENE

She watched intently, holding her breath in awe and wonderment. She watched the head protrude and then the shoulders. She saw the doctor move rapidly then and soon the whole baby was out. A new person had been born.

Later that same day she wondered how many babies had been born in the long history of man. She wondered what it had been like for mothers twenty thousand years ago. Were babies born in the back of a cave? Did mothers lie down on a pile of animal skins? Who took care of them?

He picked out a record, put it on the turntable, and sat down to listen to the stereo set. Half an hour later, he turned the stereo off, turned on the television, and watched the ball game for the rest of the afternoon. When twilight came, he turned on some lights in the room and called a friend on the telephone. That night they went to a superscreen movie. When he got home, he showered under preheated water and went to sleep under the artificial warmth of an electric blanket, breathing filtered and mechanically cooled air. In the morning, his clock-radio woke him up to the soft sounds of recorded music.

The telephone booth was made of glass, plastic, and aluminum. It stood upright, bolted to a small slab of concrete that lay solidly on the ground in the middle of the cemetery.

From a distance, the shape of the telephone booth blended with the monuments and the statuary. At a closer range, it could be mistaken for a large and shining headstone that marked the grave of a recently deceased digital computer.

One of the more important and less obvious parts of the environment in which we live consists of the ideas, thoughts, opinions, beliefs, feelings, and attitudes we have. These aspects or facets of man's immediate and personal environment have changed over the years, but not altogether.

The probability is high that thousands of years ago, mankind firmly believed in magic and witchcraft. Thunder and lightning were omens. To stub one's toe at the entrance to the mud hut may have had a secret meaning and blood may have been seen only as a fluid filled with strange and mysterious power.

The belief in magic and witchcraft faded somewhat as mankind gradually grasped the idea that there may be some greater force than he controlling the change of seasons, the movements of stars, and the birth of babies. The idea can be expressed in a number of ways. It is possible to say that man developed religion, that man invented gods, or that God revealed himself to man. In any case, magic and witchcraft faded and what is called religion received more attention.

Man's belief in gods or a God or in some unknowable but powerful force has faded since the Middle Ages and a belief in science has gradually come to the fore.

■ Science, or more accurately, science and technology, influence man's behavior to a great extent.

AGREE   (SEE PAGE 147.)

DISAGREE (SEE PAGE 149.)

Following is a *brief* list of a very few of the results or products of science and technology.

1. 1968: Discovery of the Ovshinsky effect
2. 1957: First successful launch of an earth satellite
3. 1953: Structure of DNA identified
4. 1947: Invention of the transistor
5. 1942: First large-scale atomic chain reaction
6. 1936: First successful helicopter flight
7. 1905: First writings by Einstein on the theory of relativity
8. 1894: First radio communication system used
9. 1866: Invention of dynamite
10. 1698: First practical steam engine used

Which of the products or results of science and technology on the list has influenced your life more than any of the others? Write your answer and why on a blank sheet of paper.

The question was this: Which of the products or results of science and technology has influenced your life more than any of the others listed? Few people, perhaps, would answer with "the Ovshinsky effect" because that discovery is too recent to have affected many lives. In time, it may. In time, it may change your environment in some dramatic ways. If you are curious about it, you may be interested in reading Stanford R. Ovshinsky's article in the December, 1968, issue of *Physical Review Letters.*

You may be able to follow the influence of the Ovshinsky effect on your environment over the years that lie ahead. Your environment may perhaps be changed and your life influenced by Ovshinsky's discovery.

It may be that science and technology have influenced man's behavior more than any other of man's own developments. The inventions and discoveries have brought gigantic changes to the environment and, because of that, have brought changes to man. The inventions and discoveries are often clearly identifiable, easily recognized, and useful or potentially useful in one way or another. It may be, however, that there are more critical factors than inventions and discoveries involved in the realm of science and technology. These factors that may be more critical seem to involve opinions, beliefs, feelings, and attitudes about science and technology.

■ For many people, there may be a belief in science and technology that is as strong as some other people's belief in religion.

AGREE   (SEE PAGE 148.)

DISAGREE   (SEE PAGE 150.)

Right.

Science and technology influence man's behavior to a great extent.

The world of science and technology forms only a portion of the environment in which we live. Yet, science and technology affect great portions of the total environment, and the total environment influences behavior.

While thinking about science, turn to page 145.

If you agree this time, you are correct.

Large numbers of people are fervent believers in science and technology. Many believe science will eventually answer all questions and solve all problems and technology will design and build the machines to be used in the answering and solving effort.

Many people believe science will eventually find all the right answers. They may be able to trace man's history of beliefs, pointing to the failure of magic and witchcraft, the apparent (for some) failure of religion, and the assumed or presumable success of science in providing solutions to man's problems. It is as though all the problems were "out there" in the environment.

To put it on a more basic and personal level, the belief that science will find all the answers may be similar to the belief children have that parents will always take care of everything.

In a slightly different way, the belief that science will take care of everything and eventually solve all problems may be similar to a dependence on other people rather than some appropriate level of dependence on oneself.

In an additional and again somewhat different way, an optimistic and hopeful dependence on science to solve problems may be similar to a belief held by many people, "If things were a little different, life would be better." There are many people who say this in one way or another and then sit back passively waiting for things to get better. These may be the people who prefer to travel through life as passengers rather than drivers. They are not rare.

Start the next chapter on page 151.

If you disagree with the statement, you are wrong.

It may be that science and technology have influenced man's behavior more than any other of man's own developments.

Read more about this on page 147.

If you disagree, you are wrong in this instance.

Large numbers of people are fervent believers in science, the scientific methods, the results and products of science, and the beneficial effects of technology. Some of the believers may be scientists, but many are not.

START OVER ON PAGE 146.

11

ANXIETY

He pressed his hand against his stomach, but the tight feeling inside didn't go away. His gut felt like a golf ball. He looked at the palm of his hand and saw the sweat glisten in the creases. He could feel his heart beat in his throat, and he wondered how long it would last, pounding away like that. He sucked at the air, breathing rapidly but in a shallow way. His knees seemed to be made of Jello and he wasn't sure he could walk to the front of the room to make his speech. He wondered if he could stand up.

He felt eager, alert, finely tuned and as steady and sure of himself as he'd ever been. He felt tall and strong and indestructible and he knew he was ready to go. He buckled the harness tightly to his body, stepped to the open door and leapt out of the airplane. The wind caught him and he spread his arms and legs out as he fell toward the green fields a mile below. The small black seed of anxiety that lay lodged in the back of his brain grew suddenly and burst open to show the red flower of fear. He wondered if his parachute would open. He laughed with his teeth clenched tightly together.

All people feel anxiety from time to time, and a few feel anxious almost all of the time.

For most people, the unpleasant tension, the apprehension that is called anxiety, may last for a few moments. Once in a while it may stay for several hours.

The feeling that is called anxiety is almost the same as the feeling called fear.

When a person feels fear, he will be able to name what it is he is afraid of. If the same feeling exists within him and he cannot name what he's afraid of, the feeling is called anxiety. Fear has an identifiable fear-producing object or stimulus involved. Anxiety has none.

We live in what has been called the Age of Anxiety because of the concerns many people have about war, nuclear power, computers, high-level educational requirements, competition, crime, pollution, drugs, sex, and quickly passing time, to give a few examples. Our culture is one of change, and change is frequently perceived as dangerous.

Anxiety can be brought about by change, by ambiguity and unsureness, and by threats or challenges to one's own status. Perhaps the most common causes of anxiety are threats to a person's self-worth, to his self-esteem. (Keep in mind as you move along in this chapter that the degree of anxiety a person may feel depends on the importance he places on a particular threat or situation.)

■ Which of the following examples indicates anxiety:

An unmarried young woman misses a menstrual period. (TURN TO PAGE 157.)

An unmarried young woman is told that she is pregnant. (TURN TO PAGE 160.)

A common reaction to frustration is anger, and anger has already been mentioned in this book (on page 87). Another common reaction to frustration is anxiety. There are a number of different conditions that can bring about frustration, which may be followed by the rise of anxiety within an individual. One sort of contition that may do this is called conflict.

Conflict is a type of frustrating condition in which a person must make a difficult choice betweeen goals. A common sort of conflict involves making a choice between two goals, both of which may be wanted or needed or desired by the individual. This sort of conflict is technically called an *approach-approach* conflict.

Another sort of conflict involves the choices one must make in trying to avoid two or more negative goals. These are called *avoidance-avoidance* conflicts.

■ A scientist was exploring the land near the headwaters of the Amazon River. He was alone. He was captured by fierce Indian tribesmen who tied him up to a ceremonial tree in the middle of their village. The tribesmen danced and chanted for 3 days, but then it was time to sacrifice the scientist to their god of darkness. They told him, by gestures and pantomine, that he could choose his way of death. He could jump off a 400-foot cliff or be strangled to death. The choice was his to make.

If this seems like a choice involving an avoidance-avoidance conflict, turn to page 158.

■ A nurse is taking care of a patient who is dying. She stands by his bed, holding his hand as he fades slowly away. She doesn't want to be there, but she has promised the patient she won't leave. Suddenly, there is a loud call for help from the hallway. The nurse must choose between staying with the dying patient or going out into the hallway to see what the trouble is. She must make a choice.

If this seems to be an avoidance-avoidance conflict, turn to page 161.

A third type of conflict is called the *approach-avoidance* conflict. This type comes about when the person is faced with a situation that has both positive and negative goals. An old example is the conflict the married man may feel as he watches his mother-in-law drive off a high bridge in his new Corvette. A situation such as that might give rise to ambivalence. The man might have mixed feelings about the accident.

■ The young woman puts a high value on her own freedom and independence. She likes her work and she is successful at it, but sometimes she gets lonely. If she were to get married, she believes she would not be lonely any more. The choice involves a life style that would have great personal freedom combined with some loneliness versus considerably less freedom with no loneliness.

If this seems to be an approach-avoidance conflict, turn to page 159.

■ The man is a dedicated and serious physician. His patient is in great pain, which drugs will not relieve. If he gives the patient a certain medication, the patient will live but will always be in pain. If he does not give the medication, the patient will surely die. Should he let the patient die or should he keep the patient alive but in great pain?

If this appears to be an approach-avoidance conflict, turn to page 163.

Conflicts are often frustrating. Frustration is a condition that can lead to the development of anxiety. Frustration is a condition that can lead to the development of anger.

Anxiety can develop after anger has been expressed. Anxiety can also develop after affection has been expressed openly to another person. In each case, the anxiety can rise up because of something that has already been done.

There are many instances when people will feel anxiety about feelings that do not get expressed. It is possible for people to feel angry within themselves. They may not allow themselves to openly express their anger. They may become fearful of what would happen if their anger were to be expressed. It is also possible for people to have angry feelings and not be aware of these feelings. Instead of fearing a known anger, they may feel anxious about the unknown feeling that resides within.

Anxiety can be viewed as a subtle sort of enemy of man. Anxiety can also be viewed as an unseen friend.

Anxiety motivates. If someone feels anxiety, he may become active in ways that are designed to reduce the feeling of anxiety. For instance, if someone is anxious about a grade on an examination, he may study with diligence and care in order to achieve a good grade. If a father is anxious about the welfare of his children, he may spend considerable energy in doing good things for them. If a teacher is anxious about teaching, she may spend an inordinate amount of time in careful preparation of lesson plans.

Anxiety, on the other hand, may cause a stoppage of behavior. If the student sits down to take the examination and freezes and cannot think of any answer to any of the questions, he may be almost paralyzed by a high degree of anxiety. If the father becomes too anxious about his children, he may do nothing more than sit around and worry about them. The teacher may become so anxious about teaching that she will be unable to talk sensibly while in front of her class, no matter how much preparation she has done.

From time to time in this book, you have read about the sense of personal identity. The sense of personal identity is based on and developed out of self-knowledge. To know one's own self, to be aware of one's own feelings and the elements of process, and to be able to acknowledge one's own assets and liabilities all form part of the sense of personal identity.

The sense of personal identity includes one's overall evaluation of himself. A person may be able to say, "I'm basically all right," or "I'm average," or "I am unusual and gifted," or "I'm really not much of a person." Whatever he may believe about himself, he operates somewhere along a dimension we can call self-esteem.

Self-esteem is the degree to which a person likes or dislikes himself. If an adult views himself some of the time as a child, it may be that he has a lowered level of self-esteem. He has, to use another term, a poor self-concept. If he views himself as adequate and competent in some relevant areas of living, he may have a reasonably positive level of self-esteem. His self-concept will probably be good.

■ If an individual has a solidly based level of self-esteem and a generally good self-concept, he may not be as vulnerable to anxiety as a person with low self-esteem, with a low concept of himself. (SEE PAGE 162.)

■ All people will be vulnerable to anxiety to about the same degree, regardless of their level of self-esteem and in spite of the kind or level of self-concept they may have. (TURN TO PAGE 164.)

You are already showing an understanding of anxiety. This young lady will probably be very anxious about missing a menstrual period. She may be concerned about a possible pregnancy. She may anticipate that she has a physical disorder or a serious illness. The anxiety is nonspecific, internalized.

Most people react with some anxiety to any change in body function. The developing adolescent will typically experience anxiety because of bodily changes such as the appearance of pubic hair. Older people may sense some anxiety when they discover they do not have the same physical stamina and endurance they once had. Almost everyone will feel anxiety if he is faced with surgery, no matter how minor the operation. Physical illness can bring about an increase in anxiety unless the individual can effectively defend himself against the rise of anxiety. The next chapter of the book delves into such defenses.

TURN TO PAGE 153.

You are correct. The scientist is up against an avoidance-avoidance conflict.

If he is like most people, the scientist will want to avoid death, whether it is by way of a 400-foot fall or strangulation.

Perhaps you can think of other examples of this sort of conflict. On a sheet of paper, write down an example of an avoidance-avoidance conflict you have found.

THEN TURN TO PAGE 154.

Well, the woman is in a complicated sort of conflict that involves a double approach-avoidance situation. On the one side, she can have a lot of freedom (an approachable or desired goal) but she must live with a certain degree of loneliness (an avoidable or undesirable goal). If she marries, she will lose a good deal of freedom (avoidable) but reduce her loneliness (approachable). This is a double approach-avoidance situation.

Perhaps you will remember some previous comments made in this book regarding the matter of loneliness versus involvement with other people. A common and very human conflict can develop when a person must choose between the safety of loneliness and the risky matter of trying to develop intimate relations with other people. This exemplifies the double approach-avoidance conflict.

Read about the other situation, too, on page 163. Then go to page 155.

Sorry, this woman is reacting to a specific stress, so she will feel fear rather than anxiety. The pregnancy is a reality that she must deal with. It is not an unknown factor in her life.

The words *anxiety* and *fear* are often misused because the emotional and physical reactions are so similar. Remember, if you can clearly identify the stimulus, you are experiencing fear. If the stimulus is vague and unclear, you are experiencing anxiety.

Another word that is commonly misused is *nervous*. Some people feel that "nervous" implies less emotional involvement than "anxious." Years ago, and even still, some people referred to mental illness as a nervous breakdown. Perhaps it is easier to think of broken down nerves than broken down relationships.

Return to page 152 and select the other answer.

The nurse is not involved in avoidance-avoidance conflict. She may want to avoid the close association with death, but she may not want to avoid finding out what the trouble is in the hallway. She is not involved in a balanced conflict.

Select the other answer on page 153.

You are right.

Self-esteem and self-concept are related to the ability to handle anxiety-provoking situations.

It seems that people who have a fairly sure sense of personal identity are able to handle anxiety and anxiety-provoking situations with more ease than people who have an uncertain sense of their own identities. In other words, the chances are high that the more a person knows about himself the more stress he will be able to tolerate.

Individuals with a reasonably adequate level of self-esteem and with positive self-concepts seem to be able to handle themselves well under stress. They may not become as easily anxious as individuals who have a modest level of self-esteem and low self-concepts.

Turn to page 165 for Chapter 12.

The physician is involved in a conflict that may be difficult to resolve. He may feel ambivalent about what he should do, and chances are he will feel some anxiety no matter which choice he makes.

He is faced with a double approach-avoidance conflict.

A single approach-avoidance conflict would take into account only one side of the problem the physician faces. Perhaps he could locate an exotic and rare drug that would reduce the pain. Yet, the drug would damage brain tissue and slowly kill the patient. Should he give the drug or not? What would you do? Keep in mind that if you were a physician you would have values that put a high priority on saving life and reducing pain. Here, you would be involved in a problem that is a conflict because to save a life would mean to allow the pain to continue; but to reduce the pain would involve ending a life. Take your choice. It is a situation that is bound to produce some anxiety.

Read about the other situation, too, on page 159. Then go to page 155.

Wrong.

While all people may be vulnerable to anxiety, they will not be vulnerable to the same degree. People with a well-developed sense of personal identity who have adequate levels of self-esteem and who enjoy a positive self-concept may handle anxiety and anxiety-provoking situations with relative ease. People who are in doubt about themselves, who do not know much about themselves, and who have low self-esteem and poor self-concepts may be extraordinarily vulnerable to anxiety. They may not be able to handle anxiety-provoking situations well.

NOTE: The "right" amount of anxiety varies from person to person.

Each one of us has his own set of ideas, thoughts, opinions, beliefs, feelings, and attitudes. All of these put together make up what can be called our frame of reference.

A person's frame of reference can help him determine how he views the world around him. An individual with a positive frame of reference may view the world and the people in it in an optimistic way. An individual with a negative frame may be pessimistic.

START OVER ON PAGE 156.

12
DEFENSE MECHANISMS

When he was a small boy, he was always thin and weak looking. His father tried to build up his strength and get him in shape by exercising with him and through sports. He worked hard at both, but he stayed thin and never seemed to have enough coordination to play well at anything. He knew all the rules and all the strategies for baseball and football and basketball. He knew the players and their averages and records and he became a knowledgeable spectator. When he grew up, he came to be known as the best sports reporter on the West Coast.

She was always pleasant, consistently sociable, well mannered, polite, gracious, charming at parties, and a friend to all. She amazed people with her patience and good will. She never argued, never pouted, and never became even mildly irritated no matter what happened to her. When she was forty-five years old, she died. Some people said she died from exhaustion. They said she must have been tired out from holding up that big smiling mask in front of her face all those years.

He was tired of it all, he said. Tired. He'd done his share and sometimes more than his share, but people always disappointed him. He would have no more of the hypocrisy, the cynicism, the double and triple standards, the meaningless rat race, he said. He packed a few of his things into a cardboard suitcase and hitchhiked his way to the Rocky Mountains, where he found an abandoned cabin twenty miles from the nearest road. He's probably there now, living alone, safe from other people.

Every human being is born an uncivilized savage. By means of direct orders, by way of competition, and through consultation in the family, the savage infant slowly evolves to be a reasonably civilized child.

Even the most civilized child and probably every adult must deal with the remnants of the savage that still lives within each person. At the same time, the individual must contend with the rules and regulations of the family, the school, and that large and loose organization called society. The savage and the civilized portions of each individual must somehow be kept in balance. They must be integrated.

Each person is glued together by what is sometimes referred to as the self or the ego. We behave in a more or less consistent way because the part of us that is called ego or self keeps us in balance. The ego or self is sometimes defined as the integrating part of personality. Whenever the ego or the self is threatened by forces that may push it out of balance or interfere with its integrating function, defense forces come to the rescue.

If the ego or self is unable to function in an adequate manner, the individual may not be able to function adequately enough to meet and deal with daily problems.

Most people must have ways of handling anxiety and dealing with problems before the anxiety and problems lead to the development of a sense of inadequacy. In other words, people must have ways that keep the peace within themselves and with others. Most people must protect themselves from anxiety and stress.

Defense mechanisms (sometimes called adaptive mechanisms, adjustment techniques, or coping mechanisms) are used by all of us to protect the ego from anxiety and stress. Defense mechanisms operate on an unconscious level, so we are not usually aware that we are using them.

Probably the most common of all defense mechanisms is denial of reality. We are able to evade many stressful situations by ignoring or refusing to acknowledge their existence, their reality.

One of the most common defense mechanisms is called *rationalization.* It is in use if the individual makes up "good" reasons to justify his behavior. Rationalization often involves a conscious effort to convince other people that we have wise motives for our behavior.

■ Select one of the following as an example of rationalization:

A boy spends money far in excess of his allowance because he says girls will respect him if he has plenty of money. (TURN TO PAGE 177.)

A girl tells her roommate, "I'm not going to study tonight. I think I'll round up some bridge players." (TURN TO PAGE 181.)

"She was always pleasant, consistently sociable, well mannered, polite, gracious, charming at parties, and a friend to all. She amazed people with . . ."

Do those words seem familiar? The paragraph about the amazingly pleasant lady briefly describes one sort of behavior that may show itself when repression is used as a defense mechanism. Repression masks over the real feelings a person may have.

Repression is a widely used and completely unconscious defense mechanism. Painful experiences and unacceptable thoughts and impulses are forced into the unconscious and forgotten. Repression is like an infection that has been walled off yet remains a focus of infection to poison the entire organism. It takes energy to repress thoughts, just as it takes energy to hold a handful of ping-pong balls under water.

When people are busy protecting themselves by repressing painful thoughts or desires, they often become so anxious that they fail in their normal tasks of living.

■ An example of repression is:

your forgetting the name of a person who is an old acquaintance. (TURN TO PAGE 178.)

your saying about a person, "Don't mention his name to me." (TURN TO PAGE 182.)

If a grown man were to have a tantrum, complete with yelling and crying, his actions would probably look silly or foolish, but they would not be rare.

If a woman of 25 sucked her thumb, she might seem immature to some people; but if she were engaged in a comparable and parallel activity such as smoking a cigarette, she would not look immature.

If a 16-year-old boy weeps when he does not get his way or an 18-year-old girl lisps every time she feels anxious, some people might recognize these behaviors as immature.

A few people, seeing the behaviors mentioned above, might recognize them as examples of regression.

Regression is a return to an earlier way of behaving. Regression is a temporary taking on of behavior that may have been appropriate for the individual at a much earlier age. When an individual fails to solve a problem with his usual methods, he may regress and attempt to handle the problem in the way he may have handled it years ago.

■ Choose an example of regression from the following situations:

A young wife calls her mother on the phone to ask how to cook a roast. (SEE PAGE 179.)

A woman cannot afford to buy a new dress and when she tells her husband about the problem, she cries. (SEE PAGE 185.)

Introjection was first mentioned in Chapter 1. This defense mechanism was brought into focus early in the book because it is a critically important aspect of behavior during infancy and early childhood.

Introjection involves taking in, and then accepting as one's own, all manner of items. We introject the language. That is, we learn it, take it in, use it, and the language becomes ours. At the same time, we introject beliefs, ideals, and prejudices and make them our own to the point where we defend them.

Introjection takes place during childhood, of course. However, it often takes place during the adult years as well.

The defensive strategy that brings introjection into play is the need to avoid being at the mercy of someone else's beliefs and attitudes. If those beliefs and attitudes become one's own, they are made more acceptable. They are made less anxiety provoking.

Introjection is the opposite of projection.

Projection is a commonly used mechanism of defense. It often involves a transfer of blame. Projection can also involve denial of reality, a disowning of a behavior or characteristic.

If projection involves a transfer of blame, the usual mode is to blame someone else for one's own mistakes or shortcomings. Sometimes an angry person (who may be almost totally unaware of the angry feelings he has) may believe that someone else feels angry. Anger exists in the situation, but because the person feels anxious about having anger, he may come to believe the other person is angry, not he.

Projection is used to attribute to others our own unacceptable impulses, thoughts, and desires. This mechanism is employed when ideas and impulses are too painful to be acknowledged as belonging to ourselves. When projection is used, we strongly deny having the attribute that is projected out.

Following are examples of projection:

1. A young soldier in basic training feels other soldiers are trying to seduce him. It is rather common for a young man with homosexual tendencies to have these feelings accentuated in basic training. He may find these feelings so unacceptable that he projects them on to other men.

2. A man accuses his wife of being unfaithful to him. Men who have impulses to be unfaithful may project this guilt-arousing feeling onto their wives and remain unaware of their unconscious desire.

3. A student says that the teachers are trying to prove he is crazy. In this example the student projects his feelings about being

mentally ill onto the teacher. This way he does not have to consciously believe that he is ill.

It is generally safer to throw rocks at a cat than to be involved in a fight with a grown man.

It may be easier for a woman to yell at her husband than it would be for her to yell at her father.

If the rock thrower is really angry with his brother (or some other person) but he takes his feeling out on a cat, he is displacing. If the wife feels anger toward her father, and if she believes she cannot express this feeling to him, and if she eventually ventilates the anger at her husband (or some other target), she is displacing.

In *displacement* there is a shift of emotion from one person or object, toward which it was originally directed, to another person or object. Displacement may sometimes seem similar to what is called compensation.

Compensation is common, widespread, and sometimes a productive way of dealing with anxiety and stress.

Most people do not find much pleasure in being inadequate. The first vignette of this chapter describes a person who was physically inadequate. He was unable to succeed in sports as long as he tried to be an active participant. However, he could succeed by shifting his efforts to a different kind of activity still associated with athletics. He compensated.

Compensation involves making up for a lack of success or gratification in one area by developing an increased level of success or gratification in another area.

A common example of compensation can be found in the blind person who compensates for blindness by making better use of his hearing.

Here are four brief examples of compensation.
1. The parent compensates for not being with his children much by buying them lots of games and toys and clothes.
2. The single woman compensates for a lonely home life by devoting much of her time to work.
3. The married man compensates for an unhappy marriage by devoting much of his time to work.
4. A boy compensates for loss of community acceptance by being rough, tough, and delinquent.

Compensation is sometimes confused with *sublimation*, a defense mechanism in which socially approved activities are substituted for activities not so socially approved.

There are some people who would like to be involved in a rough and bloody fight with another person once a week. If they did, however, they would be constantly in trouble with the law. Yet, the need for a physical battle remains. They must somehow handle this need. So some of these people become professional football players. Others play hockey in a professional league. They have a need for uncivilized activity, but they manage to channel their need into reasonably productive (and profitable) activities. They substitute one activity for another. They sublimate.

■ Choose one of the following situations as an example of sublimation:

A girl acts out her sexual desires by reading sexually oriented novels. (SEE PAGE 180.)

A man acts out his sexual desires by having an affair with a married woman. (SEE PAGE 186.)

Identification has already been mentioned (on page 24). You may recall that identification of the girl with the mother and the boy with the father was common behavior during the years from 7 to 11.

If a person identifies with another person, he usually takes on what he considers to be the desirable attributes of that other person.

Identification is not the same as imitation. To imitate is simply to copy. To identify is to take on and accept as one's own the behavior and the characteristics of a person who is admired and perhaps loved.

It is healthiest to identify with people who are living and in proximity to us. For example, it is usually appropriate to identify with parents and peer group members.

The purpose of identification is to enhance our feelings of self-worth and self-esteem by identifying with someone we see as positive and powerful.

Very sick people (in the old days) used to identify with Napoleon, a powerful conqueror. No one identifies with Napoleon any more. Most famous people today receive criticism, as well as praise. Therefore, emotionally ill people choose to identify with religious figures, who are considered positive and powerful yet seldom criticized.

NOTE: Emotionally ill women sometimes identify with the Queen of England. The Queen is famous but not criticized as much as strictly political leaders.

Identification is closely connected with intimacy. The opposite of the development of intimacy is sometimes referred to as emotional insulation.

Emotional insulation is an activity or behavior that is designed to reduce the degree of emotional involvement in situations that might prove disappointing. Emotional insulation is often seen in people who try to stay cool and aloof even when they are in highly emotional situations. It is sometimes the opposite of the development of intimacy.

■ Which one of the following examples involves the defensive tactic called emotional insulation:

A boy immediately begins dating again after having broken off a love affair. (SEE PAGE 183.)

A boy puts off looking for a job because he is afraid he may be turned down. (SEE PAGE 187.)

We all must contend with the savage and the civilized portions of ourselves. We must somehow keep a balance between the two by integrating the wild with the calm, the hot with the cool.

Sometimes we slip and a slight bit of the savage shows itself, and we can experience a sense of disapproval. If that happens, we typically will apologize in one way or another.

Many people learn at an early age to apologize. An apology can be made with words, with gestures, or with actions of one sort or another. Apologies are a form of undoing a mistake.

Undoing is a mechanism of defense used to make amends for some disapproved thought or act.

There are some among us who become greatly concerned with the so-called uncivilized aspects of being and these people may go well beyond simple undoing. They may develop a massive defense against making even potential mistakes. They may protect themselves against what they consider to be dangerous desires by not only repressing them but actually developing conscious attitudes and behavior patterns that are just the opposite. In this way they erect barriers to reinforce repression and keep real desires from being carried out in overt behavior. This defense mechanism of doing the opposite of what is felt is called *reaction formation.* Usually reaction formation can be easily recognized by a show of extreme intolerance, which is out of all proportion to the importance of the situation.

■ Which of the following could be an example of reaction formation:

A mother is extremely protective of her children. (TURN TO PAGE 184.)

A man is careful always to keep his apartment neat and tidy. (TURN TO PAGE 188.)

We all use defense mechanisms in ways that seem almost automatic. If someone points out that we are using a particular defense mechanism, we may defensively deny that we are doing so.

Defense mechanisms can be used to such an extreme that they interfere with rather than aid normal function.

The mechanisms of ego defense do not solve the underlying conflicts that cause anxiety. They may help us to handle the feelings that we have about a problem, but ordinarily they do not solve the problem for us.

Defense mechanisms can be categorized. Typically and normally, they fall into categories of fight, flight, and compromise.

Turn to page 176. Follow the directions there. You may need to refer to the list of mechanisms presented below.

Denial of reality	Undoing	Compensation
Rationalization	Regression	Displacement
Projection	Identification	Emotional insulation
Repression	Introjection	Sublimation
Reaction formation		

On a blank sheet of paper, write down the defense mechanisms under the correct categories.

FIGHT

FLIGHT

COMPROMISE

Chapter 13 begins on page 189.

Very good. This boy tried to convince himself that spending more money than he had was wise rather than foolish.

Rationalization has two major defensive values:

1. It helps to justify what we do and what we believe.
2. It aids in softening the disappointment connected with unattainable goals.

Sometimes softening the disappointment connected with unattainable goals is handled by telling ourselves that the goal is not worth our effort. This is sometimes called "sour grapes" rationalization.

At other times the disappointment is handled by telling ourselves that the goal is really not very desirable after all and that what we presently have will be more valuable in the long run. This is an example of "sweet lemon" rationalization.

TURN TO PAGE 168.

Repression frequently operates in this manner. It is often possible to determine that you were angry or disappointed with the person whose name you forgot.

Repression is also used to protect the ego from remembering traumatic events in childhood. We unconsciously and selectively remember experiences that were positive and self-enhancing in some way. We unconsciously and selectively forget experiences that were negative.

Read page 182 also; then continue on to page 169.

No.

It makes sense to ask the person who can help you. Asking advice is important when help is needed. Going home to mother, just because cooking discouraged the young wife could be an example of regression.

Select the other answer on page 169.

Sublimation is right.

Reading love stories is quite acceptable. Acting out promiscuously is not. Sublimation is based on the utilization of general body energy in constructive activities that indirectly reduce the tension built up around frustrated sexual or other desires.

GO ON TO PAGE 173.

Sorry, wrong number. The ego was evidently not under stress in this situation. The student did not defend her behavior. She just stated what she was going to do.

Return to page 167 and select the other answer.

You selected the answer that is an example of *suppression* rather than repression. Suppression is used if people deliberately and consciously refuse to think about unpleasant thoughts. Other examples are, "I don't want to think about it," and "I'll think about it later."

Can you think of a time you used suppression?

Return to page 168 and select the other answer.

Sorry. You are wrong.

If this were an example of emotional insulation, the boy would not date again for a long while, in order to protect himself from further hurt.

You may recall the following words:

"He was tired of it all. Tired. He'd done his share and sometimes more than his share, but people always disappointed him. He would have no more of . . ."

That paragraph in the introduction to this chapter briefly touches on the defense mechanism called emotional insulation. It is an extreme example of that mechanism.

START OVER ON PAGE 173.

You are correct.

If she is extremely protective, it is possible she is reacting against her unconscious feelings of not wanting or not liking the children. This is like the person who is especially nice to people she does not like so that they will not realize it.

Can you think of an example of reaction formation?

You are ready to go on to page 175.

Yes, it is regression. You are right.

If crying for something brought results as a child, why not try it when frustration strikes the adult?

Under conditions of extreme stress, some people regress to such an earlier stage of behavior that they cannot take care of themselves. Under some conditions of high stress, certain individuals may regress all the way back to infancy. There are some mentally ill people who use this defense against anxiety and stress.

It may be that those who consistently regress believe their failures will not be so obvious if they do regress. They may also believe that less will be demanded of them if they can manage to periodically escape from adulthood and live once again as a child, even though it is only for a short period of time.

PROCEED TO PAGE 170.

Sorry, wrong choice.

In order to use sublimation the substitute goal must be socially acceptable. Having an affair with a married woman is not socially acceptable and therefore is not a helpful defense against sexual desires. Painting pictures of nudes could, in certain circumstances, be a proper use of sublimation.

Return to page 172 and select the other answer.

This is insulation. You are correct.

If he does not ask for work, he will not be rejected. At the same time, it may be frustrating not to have a job. Tension may increase in spite of the defense.

Most people choose to become actively involved in life, risking some rejection, failure, and disappointment. Those who withdraw from competition unconsciously use emotional insulation. Emotional insulation uses up lots of energy and is not usually very satisfying.

Try writing out an example of emotional insulation that involves the use of regression.

NOW TURN TO PAGE 174.

Wrong!

Lots of people are neat and tidy, maybe because they were taught that way or because they feel more organized and in control of the situation that way. If, however, the person was compulsive about neatness and could not allow any disorder or dirt, it would seem he was forming a reaction formation against a desire to be dirty or messy.

Go back to page 174 for another try.

13

ANXIETY
AND
THE MIND

When she woke up in the morning, she stared at the ceiling and quietly wished she were dead. She wondered how she could manage to die before anyone else in the house woke up. She could, she thought, cut herself and bleed in silence. She could swallow something poisonous. Her mother would certainly cry. She smiled at the idea. Her mother would feel bad and all those other people would miss her and it would serve them right because sometimes they had been unfriendly to her. Well, that was enough of that, she thought, getting out of bed. She felt calm and at ease as she got ready for school. It was going to be a good day.

He finished painting his one hundred thirty-seventh picture. He put the caps back on the tubes of oil paint and carefully cleaned his brushes and sat down to look at the landscape he'd just completed. He didn't like it. He'd worked for six hours on the scene but he didn't like it so he threw the painting on the floor and walked out and down the street to the bar on the corner. He got drunk there for the third time that week. Someday, he thought, he would be rich and famous, but today he'd have a drink or two and find some grass he could smoke for breakfast and that was enough for now.

What frightened him more than anything else was the doctor. He didn't mind the doctor's moustache or his bow tie or the way he walked. What frightened him was the paper-doll appearance. The doctor didn't look like a person. He looked like a big paper doll cut out of cardboard, flat, with a painted-on face and eyes that looked like flat black rocks glued on. He couldn't tell anyone about the way the doctor looked to him. He didn't know what to do except to feel afraid.

There is no such thing as random behavior. There is no such thing as purposeless behavior. All behavior has meaning. Sometimes, however, we may not be able to determine what a particular behavior means.

The central theme of all behavior involves the satisfaction of a need or needs. If a behavior does not satisfy a particular need, it is abandoned and another behavior takes its place. We all function in this manner.

If all behavior has a purpose, what, then, is the purpose that underlies feeling depressed? When an individual is depressed (even if only slightly sad) he may be trying to cope with or defend against a feeling of anger. Rather than express the anger at "the thing out there," the person may unconsciously express anger at himself. Anger at one's own self usually shows up as depression.

In order to maintain a balanced sense of self-esteem and to maintain and preserve whatever he believes to be an adequate reputation, the individual may not express (or even feel) anger as often as it may be there. In addition, anger may not be expressed as often as it is felt because the penalties, real or imagined, can be too high. As a result, anger can often be turned inward on oneself and a feeling of sadness or depression can result.

To feel depressed and temporarily of little worth is common. To feel even slightly depressed, dejected, and down is to feel one form of what is called neurotic behavior. When any one of us prefers or needs to be depressed rather than cope more directly with anger, we are in what is apt to be a neurotic behavioral state.

When people are in a neurotic state, they are typically unhappy, psychologically uncomfortable, anxious, ill at ease and usually unhandy, inefficient, or simply stupid when they try to solve some of the problems that confront them.

The problems a neurotic person must handle are usually no different from the problems all people must handle. The problems are in the environment ("out there") and within the individual ("in here").

A common component of neurotic behavior is anxiety.

Anxiety is caused by stress. Stress can exist in the environment in the form of rules, regulations, expectations, and social demands. Stress also exists within the individual and it takes the form of feelings. The neurotic person may be anxious about the feelings he has. He may wonder anxiously whether he can maintain control over the feelings.

In capsule form, the person who is in a neurotic state may be anxious when he thinks about what the environment may do to him and what he may do to the environment.

Put in slightly different terms, the neurotic individual may be anxious about an environment (including the people in it) that he may believe is about to injure, cripple, or destroy him. He may be anxious about his own feelings and believe that if those feelings were to get out of control he would injure, cripple, or crush his environment and, perhaps, the people who live in his environment.

Many people become anxious about the possibility they may receive more love and affection than they care to deal with. They may, additionally, be anxious about the strength and durability of the control they feel they must have over the love and affection within themselves. They may worry lest the positive feelings break too much into the open.

■ Anxiety motivates behavior. Anxiety can motivate behavior that is designed to reduce the feeling of anxiety.

YES   (TURN TO PAGE 203.)

NO   (TURN TO PAGE 207.)

When two people get together to form an intimate relationship, feelings of anxiety may rise and fall with the ebb and flow of affection and anger.

When two people try to form an intimate bond, the relationship may gradually evolve and become a neurotic interaction.

There are several ways in which a man and a woman can relate to each other:

1. Both the man and the woman can relate as adults.
2. Both can relate in a manner that is comparable to the way in which young children relate to each other.
3. The man may relate as an adult and the woman may relate as a child. In this sort of interaction, the man acts as a father while the woman acts out the part of a daughter.
4. The man may act in the role of a child, a son, while the woman may behave as an adult, the mother.

Some relationships between men and women will vary and fluctuate over the whole range of these four possibilities. Such variable styles of interaction are not neurotic. The interactional pattern that allows the partners to fluctuate in their behavior is healthy rather than neurotic. People need freedom of movement to be what they really are rather than restrictions on behavior that may cause them to pretend.

It may be that marriages and other close relationships that follow a rigidly consistent pattern of behavior are limited relationships in which both people function with a worrisome carefulness lest they step out of line.

A person who does not fluctuate and vary his behavior may be so rigid and so inflexible as to be neurotic.

A person who consistently strives to be a calm and orderly adult may be overcivilized and overcontrolled. That person may complain, with some accuracy, that he never really has any fun.

An individual who always behaves in a childlike manner may tend to be undercontrolled and may, in a crisis, behave in unpredictable and incompetent ways.

The father-daughter relationships between adults are common. Mother-son patterns of relationships are also common among pairs of adults. Neither kind of relationship allows either person much individuality or freedom of movement if that is all there is to the relationship.

It may be that the person who functions consistently as an adult could add a new and interesting dimension to life by learning to regress. Perhaps the adult who acts out the role of a child could strive to be more genuinely an adult some of the time.

People who are involved in neurotic interactions may not change their behavior unless the situation causes them emotional pain of some sort. The emotional pain may motivate behavioral change.

Although we all possess some components of neurotic behavior, some people develop such severe neurotic reactions that their daily living becomes impaired. A few of the most common neurotic reactions are briefly discussed on this and the next few pages.

When people have an *anxiety reaction*, they react with severe anxiety to situations that would not be very stressful to others.

The reason for the anxiety is usually unclear since anxiety is caused by conflicts that are repressed.

■ Which of the following is an example of an anxiety reaction:

Debbie was so upset when Steve didn't call that she wrote him a ten-page letter expressing her anger with him. (TURN TO PAGE 204.)

Vickie was unable to go to class because she was so tired and upset. She tearfully told her roommate, "I don't know what's the matter." (TURN TO PAGE 211.)

Phobias are neurotic. A phobia is an intense, penetrating, and irrational fear. The person usually knows his fear is irrational, but he cannot ignore it.

Some of the most common phobias are as follows:

acrophobia Fear of high places
claustrophobia Fear of closed places
mysophobia Fear of uncleanliness
nyctophobia Fear of darkness
zoophobia Fear of animals

Phobias are an attempt to adjust to stress by preventing its occurrence or avoiding it. The reason for the phobic reaction has been repressed. The reason is there, but it may not be identifiable. Because of that, a phobic reaction may seem irrational, unexplainable, and (to those who do not have the phobia) outlandish.

Obsessive-compulsive reactions are common. An obsession is a persistent thought that the person realizes is irrational but that he cannot avoid. A compulsion is similar to an obsession except that it is an act rather than a thought or idea. In other words, obsessions are related to thought; compulsions are related to action.

The person obsessed by cleanliness may compulsively wash his hands every few minutes, or a boy who is obsessed by guilt about masturbation may compulsively wash his hands.

Obsessive-compulsive reactions are most often apt to be defenses against anger, sexual matters, and dependency.

■ Obsessive-compulsive persons are respected in our society.

TRUE   (TURN TO PAGE 205.)

FALSE   (TURN TO PAGE 209.)

People who are *neurotic* are typically unhandy, inefficient, or at times simply stupid when they try to solve some of the problems that confront them.

People who are *psychotic* are in more difficult circumstances.

The neurotic individual normally is in fairly good but painful contact with reality. The psychotic person has lost that contact. In addition, psychotics:

1. Show a breakdown in their organization of thoughts and feelings.
2. Have little or no awareness of the problems that face them.
3. May have delusions.
4. Are apt to have hallucinations.

If the psychotic disorder results from damage to the brain because of drugs, accidents, or disease, it is said to have an organic cause.

If there is no organic cause, the psychotic condition is said to be functional. Functional disorders are usually related to stress, tension, and anxiety.

Before going any further, make certain you know the difference between a delusion and a hallucination. Define these terms on a separate sheet of paper.

The most common type of psychotic disorder is *schizophrenia.* Schizophrenia is considered by some to be one illness with many variations. Other people think schizophrenia is a syndrome (combination of symptoms).

Schizophrenia involves a difficulty in communication. People with schizophrenia may not communicate, because they are withdrawn from other people, or else they may relate to other people in hostile or bizarre ways. The schizophrenic, if he does make an attempt to communicate, may do so in ways that will make sense to him, but, chances are, they often will not make much sense to other people. The communication (by way of words, gestures, looking, and touching) will probably be based on private meanings that come from the hidden inner world of desires and feelings. The person with whom the schizophrenic tries to communicate may not be able to decode the meanings.

Schizophrenics often have grown up in families in which the

communication was confusing. For instance, a child might ask, "What kind of cake is that?" and his mother would answer, "I baked it this afternoon." Or a boy might ask, "What time is it?" and his father would answer, "Time and tide wait for no man."

Sometimes, the disturbed communication patterns involve what is called a double bind. An example: A mother might say to her daughter, "Now, don't go out with some boy and get in trouble." If the daughter did not go out, the mother could then say, "Can't you find yourself a boyfriend? What's wrong with you?"

Schizophrenia seems to develop in families in which the relationships between members of the family are unsatisfying, stress producing, and generally disturbed.

Mothers of schizophrenics are typically (but not always) cold, controlling, demanding, and aloof. They are usually the dominant partner in the marriage.

Fathers of schizophrenics are typically (but not always) quiet, reserved, and detached. They are usually the passive partner in the marriage.

The child frequently reacts to marital problems and family problems by withdrawal. If the stress is great enough, he may develop psychotic behavior. His ego may be so weak, his defenses so inadequate or rigid, and his anxiety so great that he withdraws from the real world. It is as though the real world is too confusing, too frightening, or too complicated to deal with.

It is a far reach from an anxiety reaction to a schizophrenic disorder. A great range of behavior is included under the general term mental illness. The range extends from a mild and transitory neurosis to a severe, incapacitating, and dismal psychosis in which the individual is lost not only to the world but to himself. Within that range, there are considerable and important differences between neurotic behavior and psychotic behavior. The division between neurotic and psychotic is, however, artificial.

A severe neurosis can give the appearance of a mild psychosis. A mild psychosis may often appear to be a severe neurosis. Because of that, psychiatrists and psychologists may have difficulty in distinguishing between the two; and they will sometimes use the term *borderline condition* as an appropriate compromise.

To understand the great range of behavior included within the term mental illness, consider depression once again. Feelings of depression are common, and it may be that at one time or another all people had to contend with them.

■ Even mild depression begins with a loss. One of the many forms of loss is the temporary loss of self-esteem. Which of the following would most likely result in a loss of self-esteem:

The boy fails an examination that he really didn't study for. (SEE PAGE 206.)

The boy asks a girl he's really interested in for a date. The girl turns him down. (SEE PAGE 210.)

Involutional depression occurs during middle age. In women, it is frequently related to the menopause. Men have involutional depression, too, though it may develop later in middle age.

Middle age is a time when a person begins to realize the loss of youth. He may feel the loss of physical ability and attractiveness. He sees that his life pattern for the future is fairly well set. He may think all the effort wasn't worth it. He may have lost a loved person or a prized object.

Involutional depression may be mild or it may reach psychotic proportions. The degree of real or imagined loss will affect the degree of severity.

Some people are more prone to involutional depression than others. These people are conscientious, rigid, and perfectionistic. They tend to feel guilty very easily.

If the involutional depression becomes psychotic in degree, these people often have delusions of loss of money, that they are sinful, or that a body part is missing or distorted.

■ During middle age, marital problems are

FEW (TURN TO PAGE 208.)

MANY (TURN TO PAGE 212.)

So far in this chapter, you have read briefly about neurosis and psychosis. There is a third area of mental illness that does not quite fit into those two broad categories. It is called character disorder.

Character disorders are called personality disorders and are based on a distorted or inadequate personality development.

Character or personality disorders have to do with behavior that is usually antisocial.

People who have character disorders may show a variety of symptoms, such as alcoholism, drug addiction, unusual sexual deviations, or "paperhanging" (continually writing bad checks).

■ A person with a character disorder may be a sociopath. (An alternative term is psychopath.) The sociopath has abnormal patterns of social behavior. He does not conform to what can be called the social standards of behavior. The sociopath's activities may often be detrimental to society.

The sociopath has loyalty to no one. (TURN TO PAGE 213.)

The sociopath is loyal to his own group. (TURN TO PAGE 216.)

Sexual deviations are sexual acts that are not accepted as normal by society.

The most common sexual deviations are as follows:

homosexuality Receiving sexual satisfaction from members of the same sex

transvestism Receiving sexual satisfaction from wearing clothes of the opposite sex

exhibitionism Receiving sexual satisfaction from exposing the genitals to others, usually accompanied by masturbation

voyeurism Receiving sexual satisfaction from viewing people of the opposite sex who are naked; this is usually accompanied by masturbation

pedophilia Receiving sexual satisfaction from sexual molestation of children

zoophilia Receiving sexual satisfaction from animals

rape Receiving sexual satisfaction from forced intercourse

promiscuity Receiving sexual satisfaction from having intercourse frequently, with many different people

incest Receiving sexual satisfaction from members of the same family; incest is most common between brother and sister, least common between mother and son

■ Sexual deviates feel

SEXUALLY ADEQUATE   (TURN TO PAGE 214.)

SEXUALLY INADEQUATE   (TURN TO PAGE 218.)

In the United States, drinking alcohol is a common practice. If a person loses control of his drinking and is dependent on alcohol, he is an alcoholic.

People who become alcoholics are usually those who like what drinking does for them. Some may not enjoy the taste of alcoholic beverages, but most of them like the way they feel when they are intoxicated.

Some common reasons why people drink are as follows:

Anxiety and frustration fade away for a while.

A temporary feeling of well-being occurs.

Hostile and sexual feelings can be expressed openly.

They feel more adequate, powerful, and capable.

■ Which of the following statements is correct:

A social drinker can become an alcoholic. (TURN TO PAGE 215.)

Alcoholism is inherited. (TURN TO PAGE 219.)

Alcoholism is widespread. So is drug addiction. Alcoholism and drug addiction are problems for rich and poor, old and young, men and women. Young people, however, seem to be more involved with taking drugs of various kinds than older people.

As with sociopathic behavior, sexual deviation, and alcoholism, the more or less consistent use of drugs usually indicates an unhandy and inefficient way of dealing with anxiety and tension.

Drug addiction exists if there is:

An overpowering compulsion to take the drug.

Psychological and physiological dependency on the drug.

An increase in dosage.

Detrimental effects to self and society.

■ If you have enough will power, you will not become addicted to drugs.

TRUE   (TURN TO PAGE 217.)

FALSE   (TURN TO PAGE 220.)

Yes.

Anxiety motivates. Anxiety can motivate behavior supposedly designed to reduce the feeling of anxiety.

Which of the following ways of behaving do you use when you are faced with the feeling of anxiety?

Do you become agreeable and compliant?

Do you become aggressive?

Do you become detached, aloof, perhaps withdrawn?

NOTE: In responding to the choices above, you may feel a slight sense of anxiety, but it may be useful to keep in mind that the way you handle anxiety is learned. The methods you use in dealing with anxiety were learned from parents and/or other people who were, and perhaps still are, important to you.

You may also wish to keep in mind that your way of handling anxiety may indicate a pattern of behavior that has a great deal to do with the price you are willing to pay for acceptance by other people.

NOW TURN TO PAGE 192.

Wrong. Perhaps you forgot about anxiety. Anxiety is vague and undefined.

Debbie had a definite, specific reason for stress and she reacted to it.

Apparently she is more aggressive than compliant or detached. She handled her feelings of stress by fighting back. Others may react by flight, or running away from the problem.

GO BACK TO PAGE 193.

You are correct. You are on target.

The person who is obsessive-compulsive can be and usually is neat, orderly, prompt, complete. He gets things done. By way of his behavior, however, he may be saying, "My bad thoughts and desires cannot control me. I am beautifully controlled and in charge of myself every second of the day."

Children often demonstrate mild degrees of obsessive-compulsive behavior that, at certain ages, is not neurotic. Some children may feel proud and may sense a general feeling of relief and accomplishment if they can walk all the way home from school without stepping on a single crack in the sidewalk. (Did you ever play "step on a crack, break your mother's back"?)

Sometimes neurotic obsessive-compulsive behavior develops in ways that can lead to strange and ritualistic action. For instance, a person may feel a need to walk around a table seventeen times before going outside. Someone else may have to do thirty push-ups every time he gets ready to go on a date. Another person may have to comb her hair with care and precision every half hour all day long.

Considering the above quotation about being in control, you may be able to see that the defense mechanism called reaction formation is very much a part of obsessive-compulsive behavior.

NOW, TURN TO PAGE 195.

No.

This may involve a loss of self-esteem, but it can easily be rationalized away.

If the boy really did not study for the exam, there is a good chance he did not care much whether he did well or poorly on it. He may have been only weakly involved in the task. He may have kept himself at a safe emotional distance and avoided the risk of some loss of self-esteem.

If the boy chooses to, he can rationalize his way out. He can, however, operate in a more realistic manner and simply admit that he did not study for the test.

START OVER ON PAGE 197.

Your train has been derailed. You picked the wrong answer.

Go back, please, and read page 191 again.

Well, you are wrong.

Middle-aged people who have been married for 15 or 20 or 30 years are apt to have many problems in their marriage. While this may not always be the case, problem marriages between middle-aged couples are common.

START OVER ON PAGE 198.

Think it over. You are wrong. Obsessive-compulsive people "get things done." They love detail and are good at it.

They work hard to put any situation under control so nothing can go wrong.

READ PAGE 194 AGAIN.

Yes.

Asking for a date may be something of a slight risk, and being turned down can bring about some loss of self-esteem. The loss may be temporary and perhaps handled by rationalization, repression, displacement, or other ego defense mechanisms. If the boy was vitally interested in the girl, the sense of loss may be strong and more difficult to handle by the smooth and automatic use of one or more of the mechanisms of defense. If the sense of loss is not easily dealt with, the boy may develop a sense of anger that he may not feel he can express openly. He may, instead, express the anger inwardly at himself.

NOTE: It is typical of people with a neurotic level of depression to say such things as, "Nothing matters any more," or "Why try? Everything goes wrong anyway." In addition, people who are in a neurotic phase of depression may often be apathetic and develop constipation. They may also have difficulty sleeping (insomnia) and difficulty eating (anorexia).

Although a neurotic level of depression may be serious, and even though the individual feels quite uncomfortable, neurotic depression is moderate. It is more fully developed than a mild depression, but it is not so full blown as a psychotic depression, which can be characterized as severe.

GO TO PAGE 198.

Correct.

Vicki was reacting with severe anxiety to an unknown but stressful conflict. Since the conflict was repressed, she did not know what was causing her discomfort.

Her defense mechanisms were not controlling the anxiety, and she had both physical and emotional symptoms of anxiety.

The anxiety reaction may be a continuous response, or it may come in attacks that last for hours or days.

There are many neurotic symptoms. We all reveal some of them when we are under stress.

Whatever the neurotic symptom may be, it is related in some way to an attempt to gain or to keep love and approval.

There are individuals whose neurotic symptoms develop and grow to such an extreme that they, the symptoms, interfere with daily living.

People who are neurotic rarely become hospitalized for a mental illness. If, however, they have difficulty in meeting the demands of daily living, they may need to become involved in psychotherapy.

Psychotherapy is sometimes called "the shrink scene." One of the results of psychotherapy is the development, by the patient, of a more realistic, accurate, and useful sense of personal identity.

NOTE: Individuals who have a well-developed sense of personal identity and who have a reasonably firm ego or self may be able to tolerate considerable stress without sliding into a neurosis.

TURN TO PAGE 194.

Yes, during middle age, marital problems are many.

As people grow older, they often feel less attractive and desirable. Because each partner feels needy of attention and support, both may cease to give as much attention and support to their partner as they did at an earlier time.

It is not uncommon for the middle-aged person to become involved with someone else who gives them the attention they desire. Men are often attracted to younger women who make them feel attractive and important.

While children are at home, many couples communicate only through the children and address each other as Mother and Father. When the children leave home, "mother and father" must communicate with each other, and many couples find they no longer have anything in common except the children.

NOTE: Middle-aged people who are prone to involutional depression feel they have given to the world, community, and family and yet have received little in return. They feel they have worked while others have had fun. They want people to give to them; and they want some adventure. How does this contrast with the developmental task of middle age, which has been called generativity?

TURN TO PAGE 199.

You are partially correct. There are two types of sociopaths, the antisocial and the dyssocial.

The dyssocial sociopath has strong loyalties to his group. His group is usually one involved in activities contrary to the wishes of society.

In spite of belonging to a group, the dyssocial sociopath has few meaningful relationships with people. Both types, antisocial and dyssocial, are irresponsible in their relationships with others.

The sociopath does not show remorse, regret, or anxiety over acts against society. Because he does not show remorse, he is often rejected by society as being a "sick" person. In general, society does not understand the justification for a sociopath's pleading not guilty to a crime by reason of insanity.

The sociopath is impulsive and irresponsible in his behavior. He wants what he wants, when he wants it. He does not profit from experience. He does not learn from past mistakes.

The sociopath does not have a normal conscience. When the conscience is not developed it means the child did not have an adequate or appropriate role model upon which he could have based a sense of personal identity.

Sometimes children of ministers, policemen, lawyers and judges, doctors, and teachers act out against society. In some cases this is their revenge at the parents. They are angry at their parents, sometimes unconsciously, for giving more attention to their work than to their children.

Read page 216 also; then turn to page 200.

Wrong.

Sexual deviates do not feel sexually adequate. Although some sexual deviates are married and have families, most of them feel sexually inadequate.

Some men, for example, cannot have or maintain an erection except during a deviant sexual act.

RETURN TO PAGE 200.

You are correct. A social drinker can become an alcoholic.

If the person finds that social drinking relieves anxiety, he may begin to drink more often. Most people who drink long and hard, and steadily increase their drinking, will become alcoholics.

The following symptoms indicate loss of control over alcohol:

Blackouts (forgetting what happened while drinking)

Sneaking drinks, avoiding conversation about drinking

Hiding liquor

Changes in drinking habits and behavior

Loss of friends due to drinking

Loss of work due to drinking

Remorse and rationalization about drinking

Drinking to relieve physical symptoms

A simple test of alcoholism is to see whether you can limit yourself to one drink a day for 30 days. If you cannot, you probably have a drinking problem.

GO TO PAGE 202.

You are partially correct. There are two types of sociopaths, the antisocial and the dyssocial.

The antisocial sociopath has little feeling or warmth for others. He has loyalty to no one.

He may be charming and clever and a good companion on a superficial level. In a meaningful relationship, however, he lets others down time and time again.

The sociopath is one who does not have normal conscience development. The conscience does not develop if the child did not have proper role identity at the resolution of the oedipal stage.

In most cases the sociopath did not have an adequate parental role model. Many sociopaths come from broken homes, or homes where the family was not stable. Some sociopaths come from upper or middle-class homes where the parents were quite involved with activities outside the home and had little time for or interest in their children.

Other sociopaths have consciences that are overdeveloped. They have such a rigid conscience that they feel an intense need to be punished. These people act out against society, leave clues so they will be caught, or confess so that they will be punished.

Read page 213 also; then turn to page 200.

True is false in this case.

Although will power or caution may help in developing a resistance to taking drugs in the first place, neither will help to prevent addiction if certain drugs are taken on a regular basis.

A great many adolescents try drugs of one sort or another. In many cases, they will experience a temporary relief of psychological distress. This is not, however, a lasting or permanent form of adjustment for emotionally healthy adolescents.

Research in drug use indicates that the adolescent with a developing sense of personal identity will move on. If drugs are used at all, they will be taken in an intermittent and casual manner, more for "the fun of it" than for whatever "problem solving" they promise.

Read the correct answer on page 220.

Correct. Sexual deviates do not feel sexually adequate.

The majority of people who are sexual deviates feel inadequate, unattractive, unwanted, and sexually frustrated. Their knowledge of sex is often limited and distorted. They are not, or do not feel, potent in normal heterosexual intercourse.

Sexual deviates have not learned or accepted appropriate role identity. They have locked onto a pattern of behavior that may be appropriate for an earlier stage of development.

For some, sexual deviation is a way of expressing angry and hostile feelings. For others, it is a way to strike back at family and community. For still others, it is the only way they know to seek warmth and acceptance and thereby reduce feelings of loneliness or somehow escape from the fear of loneliness.

TURN TO PAGE 201.

Sorry, alcoholism is not inherited.

There is still much to be learned about alcoholism, but evidence does not indicate that alcoholism is inherited. Alcoholism may occur in families because it is a learned adaptive response to stress. Children learn from parents or other adults important to them.

An old saying maintains that drunkards are bums and alcoholics are rich folks. Actually alcoholism is very democratic. People of all classes develop alcoholism.

It seems that people who are immature, passive, and dependent are more apt to become alcoholics than other types of people. These persons are very sensitive to criticism, have a very low tolerance for frustration, and live with almost constant tension and anxiety.

Most alcoholics, while drinking, cause problems for their families, employers, and communities. Their acting out through drinking is a social problem.

If you want to know more about alcoholism, contact the local Alcoholics Anonymous organization. Visitors are welcomed at some of their meetings; in fact, many AA organizations welcome visitors at weekly meetings.

START OVER ON PAGE 201.

False is true in this situation. Will power does not prevent physiological addiction if you take the following drugs on a regular basis: morphine, codeine, heroin, meperidine.

Other drugs such as marijuana, tranquilizers, barbiturates (sleeping pills), and amphetamines (pep pills) are habit forming but are not necessarily addictive in a physiological sense.

Physiological addiction exists if the person must have a dose of the drug on a regular interval, to avoid withdrawal symptoms.

People use marijuana for about the same reasons that they use alcohol. Both can provide:

A temporary sense of power, capability, and adequacy.

Relief of anxiety and tension.

Revolt against family and society.

Reduction of group pressure to participate.

Other reasons for consuming marijuana that are not quite so related to drinking alcohol are:

Thrill seeking.

Curiosity.

Search for creativity.

Search for insight into inner self.

The next chapter begins on the following page.

14

ANXIETY
AND
THE BODY

She lived with her husband in a sleek town house with a triple-filtered air conditioning system. She hated lint, dust, and flowers. She never went near a park or a food store, but she liked to spend her afternoons browsing in calm and fashionable shops with thick carpets and mechanically regulated atmospheres. Whenever she went out or came home, she drove quickly and nervously through traffic with all the windows of the car rolled up tight. Once, when she came home late in the afternoon, she walked into the town house living room and saw her husband standing there holding a huge bouquet of red roses. Her eyes watered instantly and she felt her chest contract in a violent allergic reaction. She screamed at him—didn't he know about her allergies?—and then she began to sneeze and gasp for air. He laughed gently then and showed her the flowers were made of plastic. She fainted.

He knew it would come to this. He knew sooner or later he'd end up here and he knew he'd be as afraid as he was now. That's what happened to men like him. He'd read about it and talked with a few people and he knew someday the pain would grow and he'd see a doctor about it and the doctor would pack him off to the hospital for the operation. Well, he'd made it.

He looked at the brilliant overhead lights of the operating room and wished the surgeon would hurry up. He was a patient man, he thought to himself, but a busy one and the sooner the operation began, the sooner it would be over and the faster he could get back to work. They needed him there and he needed to be there because he enjoyed the challenge and the power of his job.

A green-masked doctor touched him gently on the shoulder and told him to relax as he put the dark anesthetic mask over his mind. He breathed deeply and for a fleeting golden moment, he remembered how someone had loved him once. Where had all that gone?

When anxiety and stress cannot be dealt with successfully by defense mechanisms or physical activity, they may cause malfunction or disruption of the physiological balance of the body. The resulting imbalance is called a *psychophysiological* or *psychosomatic* disorder. Both terms refer to the interrelationship of psychological and physiological functioning of the body. They are labels put on disorders that seem to have an emotional basis as well as an organic basis.

It is common to experience a physical reaction to anxiety. Here is a partial list of the reactions:

Pounding heart	Headache	Rapid pulse
Tense muscles	Backache	Neckache
Dryness of throat	Diarrhea	Perspiration
"Butterflies" in stomach	Nausea	"Heartburn"
Trembling	Fatigue	Constipation
Frequency of urination	Clammy skin	Restlessness
Difficulty sleeping		Lack of appetite

These are the most common physical symptoms, but there are more as well.

If no relief from anxiety occurs, the body continues functioning on emergency level and eventually genuine damage to tissues and organs of the body occurs. The disorder may become so severe as to be life threatening.

No one knows exactly why a particular system of the body responds to anxiety and stress in a pathological way. However, it seems to be due to a combination of the following factors:

1. Type and severity of anxiety
2. Previous weakness of that physical system through heredity, accident, or illness
3. Symbolic meaning of the physical system to the particular individual
4. Secondary gain of the unconsciously selected disorder (attention and sympathy as a result of the illness)
5. Personality patterns of the individual

■ Social class membership also influences the type of psychophysiological disorder incurred.

TRUE (TURN TO PAGE 225.)

FALSE (TURN TO PAGE 228.)

Since the focus of this book is on personal and social adjustment, it may be relevant to learn about the kind of person who attempts to adjust to anxiety and stress through psychophysiological disorders.

In a majority of cases, this person has problems of dependency and insecurity. He has never learned how to handle anger or anxiety effectively, and he may tend to overreact to stress that others would deal with easily.

■ This person is most likely to have come from a family where

the father was dominant and the mother passive. (TURN TO PAGE 226.)

the mother was dominant and the father passive. (TURN TO PAGE 229.)

Certain psychophysiological disorders occur in people with particular personality needs. These needs are unconscious.

For example, asthma, diabetes, obesity, hay fever, abdominal discomfort, dermatitis, and acne are often found in persons who have a strong need for maternal protection and comfort.

Those persons who suffer from chronic insecurity may develop impotence, frigidity, enuresis, and menstrual difficulties.

When repressed hostility is the main problem, colitis, migraine headache, backache, hypertension, arthritis, and sore throat may develop.

Although each disorder has a particular meaning for the individual, all aspects of selection of the illness may be unconscious.

If one disorder does not meet the attempted adaptation need of the person, other disorders often occur. (All behavior has a purpose.)

Migraine headache, rheumatic arthritis, and hypertension frequently develop in the same individual.

These persons tend to have a history of chronic hostility and resentment. In their youth they channeled hostility into sports or other activities, but as they grew older, they could no longer do this. They have difficulty knowing how to express and admit to anger. They tend to control others through their illness.

Relieving the physical symptoms of one illness only leads to another if the stress that caused the illness is not treated as well. Put in other terms, a physical illness may be a symptom of emotional disturbance. It may be more appropriate to treat the disturbance rather than a series of symptoms that appear as physical disorders.

The annoying common cold does not develop every time a person is exposed to cold germs. It frequently develops when the person is fatigued, or run down due to emotional stress, or anxious about some coming event. The next time you have a cold, try to identify the stress factor.

Actually all illnesses have an emotional component, even cancer: it has been found that the loss of a loved person or object often precedes the onset of a malignancy. Research is also being conducted to determine how the emotions affect tooth decay.

■ Psychophysiological disorders are "all in the head."

TRUE   (TURN TO PAGE 227.)

FALSE   (TURN TO PAGE 230.)

You are correct.

Social class membership does seem to influence the type of psychophysiological disorder a person may develop.

People of the lower classes are more prone to develop such disorders as rheumatoid arthritis, hypertension, and obesity.

Those in the upper classes have more occurrences of colitis, hay fever, migraine headache, and allergies.

Psychophysiological disorders of all types are common among middle-class persons who are under much pressure to achieve socially, economically, and occupationally. Peptic ulcers are widely known as a psychophysiological disorder because of the prevalence of ulcers in men and women who have intense work pressure in the effort to achieve more socioeconomic status.

Social class may also be related to the type of mental illness an individual might develop. People in the lower classes are more prone to psychotic conditions, middle classes to depression, and higher classes to neurotic disorders.

GO DIRECTLY TO PAGE 223.

Sorry. This is not the most common family pattern.

Return to page 223 and select the other answer.

Very wrong, although it is a common bit of folklore.

Psychophysiological disorders are caused in part by anxiety and stress. However, the disorder causes actual physical change and the pain and discomfort produced are very real.

Go to page 231 if you want to know the difference between psycho-physiological disorders and hypochondriasis.

Your false answer is false.

Current studies show that social class membership does have influence on the type of psychophysiological disorder developed by an individual.

Read page 225 next and determine whether the information presented is similar to what you have noted in your neighborhood.

You are correct.

Persons with psychophysiological disorders frequently come from families where the father is passive and the mother is dominant.

In addition, the mother may often be overly protective of the child and not allow him to admit to or deal with anger and anxiety. Thus the child has to repress hostility.

You are now ready for page 224.

This is a familiar statement but it is incorrect.

Pain caused by psychophysiological disorders is every bit as severe as pain caused by strictly organic disorders. In spite of an emotional origin, actual change takes place in body tissues and organs.

GO TO PAGE 231.

Hypochondriasis is an unconscious effort to adjust to anxiety and stress. It differs from psychophysiological disorders in that no change occurs in body tissues or organs.

Hypochondriacal persons are overly concerned with physical complaints and are very anxious, insecure individuals.

When their pleas for understanding and help are ignored, the symptoms increase. Again, unless the reason for the symptom is dealt with, the symptom will increase or others will develop.

Whether the person reacts with hypochondriasis or with a psychophysiological disorder, sickness is often a means of avoiding problems. At other times, the secondary gain is to win attention and sympathy, or control others, through the use of symptoms.

REFERENCES

American youth: its outlook in changing the world (a special issue), Fortune Magazine, vol. LXXIX, no. 1, January, 1963.

Belliveau, Fred, and Richter, L.: Understanding human sexual inadequacy, Boston, 1970, Little, Brown & Co.

Berrill, N. J.: The person in the womb, New York, 1968, Dodd, Mead & Co.

Bouchard, T. J., Jr.: Personality, problem-solving procedure and performance in small groups, Journal of Applied Psychology Monograph, vol. 53, no. 1, part 2, February, 1969.

Brammer, L. M., and Shostrom, E. L.: Therapeutic psychology, Englewood Cliffs, N. J., 1960, Prentice-Hall, Inc.

Coleman, James: Abnormal psychology and modern life, Chicago, 1964, Scott, Foresman & Co.

Coopersmith, Stanley: Studies in self-esteem, Scientific American, vol. 218, no. 2, pp. 96-106, February, 1968.

Coopersmith, Stanley: The antecedents of self-esteem, San Francisco, 1967, W. H. Freeman & Co.

Croake, James W.: Adolescent fears. Adolescence, vol. II, no. 8, pp. 459-468, Winter, 1967-1968.

Curtis, C. Michael: Taking students seriously, The Atlantic, vol. 223, no. 5, pp. 101-104, May, 1969.

Dennis, L. B.: Psychology of human behavior, Philadelphia, 1967, W. B. Saunders Co.

Duffus, R. L.: Nostalgia, U.S.A., New York, 1962, W. W. Norton & Co., Inc.

*Eiseley, Loren: Science and the unexpected universe, The American Scholar, pp. 415-429, Summer, 1966.

Erikson, E. H.: Identity; youth and crisis, New York, 1968, W. W. Norton & Co., Inc.

Francoeur, Robert T., editor: The world of Teilhard, Baltimore, 1961, Helicon Press, Inc.

Fromm-Reichmann, Frieda: Loneliness, Psychiatry, vol. 22, no. 1, pp. 1-15, Baltimore, 1959.

Ghiselli, E. E.: Interaction of traits and motivational factors in determination of the success of managers, Journal of Applied Psychology, vol. 52, no. 6, pp. 480-483, December, 1968.

Gilula, M. F., and Daniels, D. N.: Violence and man's struggle to adapt, Science, vol. 164, no. 3878, pp. 396-405, April, 1969.

Goodman, Paul: Like a conquered province: the moral ambiguity of America, New York, 1967, Random House, Inc.

Heschel, Abraham, Jr.: Who is man? Stanford, Calif., 1965, Stanford University Press.

Hoebel, E. Adamson: Anthropology: the study of man, New York, 1958, McGraw-Hill Book Co.

Holloman, J. H.: The U.S. patent system, Scientific American, vol. 216, no. 6, pp. 19-27, June, 1967.

Horton, P. B., and Hunt, C. L.: Sociology, New York, 1968, McGraw-Hill Book Co.

---

*We wish to thank Loren Eiseley for having written an elegant and beautifully formulated essay on men and science.

Iverson, Marvin A.: A factor analysis of anger ratings assigned to five classes of motivational situations, Psychological Monographs, vol. 69, no. 15, pp. 1-16, 1955.

Jackson, Don D.: Schizophrenia, Scientific American, vol. 207, no. 2, pp. 65-71, August, 1962.

Kneller, Geo. F.: The art and science of creativity, New York, 1965, Holt, Rinehart & Winston, Inc.

Laing, R. D.: Knots, New York, 1970, Pantheon Books, Inc.

Lear, John: Spinning the thread of life, Saturday Review, pp. 63-66, April 5, 1969.

Lewis, Jerry M.: Family homeostasis: a view from an adolescent service, Adolescence, vol. III, no. 12, pp. 447-452, Winter, 1968-1969.

Mager, R. F.: Preparing objectives for programmed instructions, San Francisco, 1962, Fearon Publishers, Inc.

Masters, W. H., and Johnson, V. E.: Human sexual response, Boston, 1966, Little, Brown & Co.

McClelland, David C.: The achieving society, New York, 1968, The Free Press.

McGregor, Douglas: The human side of enterprise, New York, 1960, McGraw-Hill Book Co.

Michener, James A.: The quality of life, Philadelphia, 1970, J. B. Lippincott Co.

Morgan, C. T., and King, R. A.: Introduction to psychology, New York, 1966, McGraw-Hill Book Co.

Moustakes, C. E.: Loneliness, Englewood Cliffs, N. J., 1961, Prentice-Hall, Inc.

Offer, Daniel, and Sabshin, Melvin: Normality, New York, 1966, Basic Books, Inc., Publishers.

Rogers, Dorothy, editor: Issues in adolescent psychology, New York, 1969, Appleton-Century-Crofts.

Schlesinger, A. M., Jr.: The crisis of confidence: ideas, power and violence in America, Boston, 1969, Houghton Mifflin Co.

Servan-Schreiber, J. J.: The American challenge, New York, 1968, Atheneum Publishers.

Sontag, Susan: Styles of radical will, New York, 1969, Farrar, Straus & Giroux, Inc.

Spitz, Rene A.: The first year of life, New York, 1965, International Universities Press.

Stagner, Ross: Corporate decision making: an empirical study, Journal of Applied Psychology, vol. 53, no. 1, part I, pp. 1-13, February, 1969.

Sutermeister, Robert A.: People and productivity, New York, 1963, McGraw-Hill Book Co.

Szasz, Thomas S.: The uses of naming and the origin of the myth of mental illness, American Psychologist, vol. 16, no. 2, pp. 59-65, February, 1961.

Tannenbaum, A.: Control in organization: individual adjustment and organizational performance, Administrative Science Quarterly, no. 7, pp. 236-257, 1962.

Watson, James D.: The double helix, New York, 1968, Atheneum Publishers.

Wolstanholme, Gordon, editor: Man and his future, Boston, 1963, Little, Brown & Co.

Wyckoff, Jerome, editor: The Harper encyclopedia of science, New York, 1963, Harper & Row, Publishers, vols. I, II, III, IV.